TAKING BACK THE NIGHT

Matthew Oliver

Taking Back

The Night

A Call for a Warrior Generation to Arise

Copyright © 2008 by Matthew Oliver

All rights reserved. No part of this work may be reproduced, stored in a retreival system, or transmitted in any form or by any means without prior written consent from the copyright owner, except for non-profit educational purposes as stipulated by 'fair use' under section 107 of US Copyright law. All Scripture quotations, unless otherwise indicated, are taken from the New King James Version®. Copyright © 1982 by Thomas Nelson, Inc. Used by permission. All rights reserved. Scripture marked NIV taken from the HOLY BIBLE, NEW INTERNATIONAL VERSION®. Copyright © 1973, 1978, 1984 International Bible Society. Used by permission of Zondervan. All rights reserved. Please note that the name of the devil or satan will not be capitalized, as he does not merit this mark of respect. Some names have been changed to keep the identities private and to respect the individuals represented.

For more information on Club Retro mentioned in the book please visit: www.clubretro.net

Cover design by SuzetteAllen.com

For Worldwide Distribution, Printed in the USA

Dedication

In all that has been said and done, all that has been spoken and seen, all that has been dreamt and desired, I would not have tasted any of it, had it not been for my best friend, my partner, and my great joy – my wife.

We have laughed, loved and cried through it all; what fun it is pursuing destiny together. Thank You.

Thank You

Allow me to say "Thank you" to all of those who made this life-revelation possible. Thank you to those who are hungry and longing for something real, and who would not settle for anything less; you stirred passion in me and caused me to long for more.

Thank you Club Retro, "Where Hardcore Rocks", and the whole team, who have stood like a mighty army with me through everything. Steve Villar for not settling. Tadd, Robert, & Blake, for being best friends, comrades, and amazing musicians. Jamie & Estora for warring with us. Andrew & Chere for keeping us from giving up. Mom and Dad for supporting us through everything we have done and being there for us through it all. FCC for being a great home base.

Jon and Suzette "Allen" Yoshinaga for the cover artwork, all the Club Retro and CONSECRATED pictures, and for being friends.

Daniel and Katherine Martin for all the editing work, proofing and layout, and for being friends.

A big thank you to all who have supported Siobhan and me through the years. This book is a testimony of so much we have been through and the greatness of our God.

Praise for *Taking Back the Night*

I am rocked, wrecked, inspired, my hair is standing on end, my heart is a wreck and my mind is on total tilt. I have just finished *Taking Back the Night*. In a world of oversaturation it takes something pretty significant to move me. In an hour when just about everybody with a blog or a cell phone is a prophet of some sort – this young man has a message... a real one. I have just had one of these encounters he says we all are so in need of. Thank you, Matt. I'm in. Let's take back the night.

Taking Back the Night cuts both ways, bleeds love and calls out with a clear voice of conviction that is as infected with the real Jesus as anything I have ever encountered. What I know is that Matt Oliver & his amazing family can back up every breath of this book. As much as it is a call to those who have lost their way, it is also a call to those who stand in the way of invasion by the God who died to save our dying next generation. You have never fully understood the terrible events in Sodom & Gomorrah or what went on between God and Abraham until you've heard Matt break it down. Matt wields his sword (the pen) powerfully on every page–*Taking Back the Night* is his own testimony. I pray you will take this encounter in.

Bonnie Chavda
All Nations Church
Watch of the Lord

We live in the greatest hour of history! Revival is exploding around the world and here in America. Recently, the Lord spoke to me and said, "Power has been lost in the church but it is being restored when you go out." In John 10:38 it says that Jesus was "sanctified and sent into the world." We live in an hour where God is setting His people apart and sending them into the world to see cities impacted and nations discipled. *Taking Back the Night* is a clarion call for the church to once again see power restored in their cities by going outside the four walls to impact those who have never had an encounter with the love and power of God.

Matthew Oliver, in a challenging and inspiring way, calls us to give ourselves for what is burning on God's heart – lost and broken people. Matthew doesn't just challenge us but also equips us to engage in the greatest outpouring in all of history. This book is not just theory, but has been birthed out of years of effective and powerful ministry in the Sacramento area. I believe this timely book will be used to rally a generation to become the new breed of revivalists God is going to send into the darkest plagues to stand between the dead and the living and see the Kingdom of God established. This book is not one that you will be able to read casually, so get ready because once you open the pages of this book you will no longer be able to go back to "life as normal."

Banning Liebscher
Jesus Culture Director
Bethel Church in Redding, California

In America the church is losing ground through boredom and irrelevancy. That cannot be said about the work of Matthew and Siobhan Oliver. What they are doing is just as they write – they are "Taking Back the Night". Their message is a wake up call to everyone to fulfill their own calling and destiny. Capturing God's heart for this critical hour, this book will change your view of the night and stir a passion in you to walk out your prayers – to lay hold of our promise. It's a must read for leaders and for every believer who wants to make a difference about the darkness which surrounds us all. We recommend Matthew and his great new book – "Taking Back The Night".

Wesley and Stacey Campbell
RevivalNOW Ministries and Be A Hero

Matt writes from the heart. A heart of passion, but one that is informed with a perception shaped by the love of Jesus for this world. As you read you will be challenged, but more than that, you will be encouraged to think outside the box, to imagine a people who are in touch with a Jesus who is alive, and who live and act from that belief.

A man of integrity, he has provoked me to seek God not just so that love connects me to people, but that a release of God's power brings about their transformation. He communicates a hope of a new generation rising. Read the book and you will be inspired to be part of that generation.

Martin Scott
UK author of *Gaining Ground*
and *Impacting the City*

As we read the pages of our son's book, *Taking Back the Night*, we are deeply challenged by its visionary and prophetic call to arms.

Matt represents a generation of sons who live in the extreme – radical and passionate for God. They are calling us to take back that which has been lost and to re-open gates that have been closed. It is a strong appeal to us all, young and old, calling the Church of Jesus Christ to a total revolution in the way we think of church, our call and our mission – Taking Back the Night.

As a mom and dad, we believe this is a NOW WORD for us all as we move forward to claim our destiny in a time of world-wide shaking, Matt is both calling us, and showing us how, to be that dynamic, Spirit-empowered Church that is at the heart of HIS unshakable kingdom.

Richard and Lindy Oliver
Pastors, Family Christian Center
Overseers, The River

Contents

Part 1: A Call into the Night — 1
The Mohawk Challenge — 3
Beyond the Four Walls — 7
Driving with the Lights On — 13
Being Salty — 17

Part 2: Venturing into the Night — 27
Entering Uncharted Waters — 29
God Wants to Kill You — 37
Pressing in for Power — 43
Perpetuating Insanity — 51
The Most Powerful Weapon — 55

Part 3: Bringing an Encounter — 59
An Inconvenient Truth — 61
The Power of an Encounter — 65
Desperation Moves the Heart Of God — 75
Supernatural Expectancy — 79

Part 4: Transforming the Night — 91
A Love Encounter — 93
The Power of Presence — 97
The Revival Formula — 101
Heaven on Earth — 109
The Power of Waiting — 113

Part 5: A New Breed of Warriors — 115
A Chosen Generation — 117
The Living Dead — 119
Blood Thirsty — 127
An Extreme Generation — 131
The Forever Generation — 141

Part 6: Shine — 143
Becoming an Extremist — 145
Matchless Potential — 149
The Army is Rising — 153

PART 1
A CALL INTO THE NIGHT

The sun has set and we did not fear
as the dark of night descends,
for in us the light we bear as the war of wars begins.

- 1 -
THE MOHAWK CHALLENGE

It started like so many things do, out of lack. I was sitting in front of our venue, Club Retro, which had just recently opened, staring into the eyes of a young man who would change my life. He was not a pastor, not a minister, not even a kid in our youth group, but my encounter with him would transform me forever. He sat there, a cigarette firmly placed between two fingers, shaking in the cold as he took one long drag. A multi-colored Mohawk stood straight up on top of his head, which was a mass of dully-colored tattoos.

I was out of my element. I had grown up in the church. Sure, I had gone on the outreaches, the mission trips. I had attended public school, and may even have had friends who did not know the Lord. That was not what made this time different.

Here I was, on the steps to our club, telling this young man about the Lord. And he was searching, he said so himself. "I am not looking for church; I am looking for something real." His words caught me by surprise.

So I began the pitch. I started out with what I knew. God loves you. I told him that though this world may offer you false hopes and deceptive promises, God loves you no matter what.

Taking Back the Night

He would never leave you or forsake you.

He turned to me with a blank, hopeless stare. His eyes were a deep abyss lined with dark mascara, "I don't need love. My parents love me, and I hate them." He flicked his cigarette. Strike one. But I continued. "Yes, but Jesus died on the cross for you." I told him about the great price that Jesus paid, and the sacrifice He gave. That it did not end there; He rose from the grave three days later. All for him, a sinner.

"I am not stupid," he said. "I know the stories and I went to church as a kid. I am glad Jesus died; I would have killed Him myself."

What? I was scrambling. I had never heard anyone say that before. Here this punk kid sat, smoking his cigarette, staring my offer of Christ in the face and declining it, yet he had professed to be seeking something real. Here it is! I have it here!

I dug deep into the principles of leading someone to Christ. Yes, this one already knew he was a sinner. Yes, he was searching for something real. But what would it take?

I offered him the third item. Eternal life. "Christ loves you," I said. "He died on the cross for you. And He wants to give you eternal life." Here it was – the full package deal, life after death. This was all I had, my arsenal.

As Christians we are taught the three rules of salvation. Jesus loves you, He died for you, and He wants to give you eternal life. I had done my job. This young man, who was searching for the truth, had just had it all laid out before him. Years of Bible School at its best.

I cannot forget what happened next. He did not smile or smirk. He looked at me with those sad eyes and said, "What good is eternal life if I am not dead yet?"

I sat there with my polo shirt tucked tight into my crisp

The Mohawk Challenge

blue jeans, a smile on my face. And he looked at me with blank blue eyes. He took one last drag on his cigarette and crushed it under the sole of his boots. Then he grabbed my hand and stared deeply at me.

He pulled my hand and placed his hand firmly in it, palm up. "If you can show me your God right here, right now, I'll believe." A tear ran down his face. This was real.

"If you can show me your God right now, let me experience Him right now, then I'll do it, I'll give all to Him, otherwise it is just another sham."

That was the night that changed my life.

I have always believed in the supernatural. I am one who likes to push the edges, the boundaries. But there I sat with this young man, all tattooed and pierced, with Mohawk hair, unable to do anything.

What did he want from me?

What was I supposed to do?

I left there that night ruined. I had offered him all that I had and it was not enough. He wanted something more; he wanted something real. He wanted a tangible, manifestation of the power of God, and I was unable to deliver.

I remember going home that night and meeting with God, and my words sounded much like that of the young man's. I laid my hand out and I asked God to meet me there. I realized I had great words and powerful concepts. I am a natural born seller, but an awful liar. I did not have what that young man was looking for, and I wanted it. I wanted it for me. I found I was looking for the exact same encounter he was looking for, and yet I was saved.

Over the next few months I cried out to God; I cried out for something real. And God met me. But it wasn't just for me.

Taking Back the Night

God was asking me to go back. Meet that young man, that generation that lives in the dark, and give them an encounter they won't forget. And that is what He is asking of His church, His Bride.

- 2 -

BEYOND THE FOUR WALLS

The devil is not choosy; he will take what the Christian world gives him. He does not have to be choosy when we have offered up so much to him on a silver platter. No, we have not intentionally given territory away to the enemy. We did not have a game plan of concession. What we have done is set up a lifestyle of Christian living, which accepts give and take. We have determined that we cannot possibly take every area that the devil currently occupies away from him, and keep it, while growing and maturing the areas that we currently hold.

So we decide. We look the world over and we throw the thrust of our energy in one direction. There is power in unity, right? So we join forces and instead of possibly failing in many areas with no victories, we become victorious in one area and determine that God will have to deal with the rest, or we will get to it when we have time, energy or a passion.

The problem is that that day never comes, because in making a lifestyle of Christian living, we become comfortable with success, and the thought of pushing into new, uncharted waters is not appealing; in fact, it threatens our very way of life. So the devil continues to inhabit the areas we have not yet

Taking Back the Night

ventured into, or have forfeited.

These are the things we have turned a blind eye to. Things we do not like, things we do not understand, things we are constantly waiting for someone else to be called to, to have a passion for. These are the things we give the devil, unknowingly, passively. When I close my eyes and lay my head on my comfy pillow, I pray for sleep; I invite the comfort behind the solid walls of my church building, and as night falls, I pretend all is well behind the closed doors.

We have lulled ourselves to sleep with full bellies engorged on sweet words that have gone down easily. We have laid down our weapons of warfare for the safety of our blankets pulled up close around us and keeping us warm. All the while, as we pray for day, hiding in our safety, a war wages around us, and the few warriors that have ventured into the unknown, fight to take back what was never supposed to have been given away.

These warriors are not bred of the traditional church; they buck the trend of religion. When asked to sleep, instead they head off into the unknown with only one thought on their mind – who is going to fight, who is going to take back the night?

And why would the church want to venture out of its closed doors? The night does not invite it. The creatures of the dark do not long for day; they do not long for light. They have purposely hidden themselves from God, and when they are good and ready they will risk coming into the day and find what Christ has waiting for them. At least this is what we have believed. This is the lie that we have bought into.

If Christ's plan for salvation were a building, the church being its four walls, and the master plan opening its doors, then Scripture would have been written differently. It would say, 'go

Beyond The Four Walls

into all the world and build multi-million dollar complexes and open their doors. Then the unsaved will flock to the buildings, the programs, the speakers, and then they will get saved'. Of course, that was not the master plan, but it is what we have done.

Instead the Bible says, "go into all the world and preach the good news", "baptizing them in the name of the Father, the Son and the Holy Spirit" (Mark 16:15, Matthew 28:19). So where do we preach the good news? In all of the world. Not our bubble world of Christianity that we have made. We must invade their bubble, invade their world.

Out of desperation, pure fanatical desire, the world has been knocking on the doors of the church, begging for an encounter. Much like that young man, they are staring us in the face and asking for something real. But we are so afraid, afraid that we might not have it ourselves. It challenges our very beliefs and causes us to realize that it is not just about us; there is a greater picture.

> **How do you know if you are shining unless you are standing in darkness?**

At one church I worked at, we had a street ministry. On Saturdays we would hold Sidewalk Sunday School. I would go out on Saturdays with a team and meet the world around us, the unsaved, the dying, the needy.

I remember meeting these children in tough situations. Children from broken homes, homes where their parents did crack in the front room. Homes where there was only one bedroom and the mom would have a different man in the house every night, and only a sheet divided the children from her

TAKING BACK THE NIGHT

actions. Homes where the children had lice crawling in their hair. The few moments of attention we gave them on Saturdays were their only relief from the family deficiency they experienced for months on end.

I remember the first time some of these children tried to invade our bubble. It was a Sunday morning and our children's church was getting underway. We had a large group of children, a few hundred massing, and my arm was grabbed by one of our children's workers. "Matt" they said, "What are we going to do with this?"

"This," I found out, was a group of the young African American children that we worked with every Saturday, crowding outside the double glass doors to our children's church. Every Saturday we met them on their turf; now in desperation they stood, longing for more.

I went to invite them in; these were children I had relationship with. They were far from perfect, but they were hungry. As I was heading out there, the children's pastor stopped me. "Matt" he said "They cannot come in here. Their church is on Saturdays."

I couldn't believe what I was hearing. This wasn't some segregation. This was worse than that. "Why?" I asked when I could finally spit it out. "Because," he said. "They live in a world different from ours, and I am not going to let my twelve-year-old daughter sit next to some eight-year-old boy who knows more cuss words than I do." He went on, "These kids have seen more stuff than they show on the average television. And what kind of church would it be if our children go home telling their mom what cuss word they learned in church?"

Pretty convincing. Convincing if you are scared of the world. I am not afraid of the world infecting me. As one of the newly

Beyond The Four Walls

saved Christians that came from the dark of night recently told me, "Matt, it is our job to infect the night."

We have a plague, an extremely volatile virus called the good news. It spreads like wild fire and all of us have been infected. And instead of looking for a cure, or a way to coexist with the world without infecting it, we should be looking at ways to plant ourselves in the middle of society and spread this plague.

You are the light of the world, a city on a hill that cannot be hidden. How do you know if you are shining unless you are standing in darkness?

It is our job to minister to those children. I am not afraid of their sin getting in me; I know that my God is going to get in them. That is the promise I have, that is the faith I stand on.

When we started Club Retro in our old Sanctuary building, we were backed by loads of support, and opposed by some church members. One of them was a board member.

Sitting at dinner one night with him and his wife, they pleaded with us to close the club and ask for forgiveness. We will pay for allowing sin into the church, they said.

Well, I don't believe the church is four walls, just another building; we are the church. And I am not afraid of the devil. On a weekly basis we have hundreds of unsaved flocking to our church building, not for some message, or some great sermon, but for an encounter. We have the power of the resurrection blood living in us, the light of Christ. Now shine!

- 3 -

DRIVING WITH THE LIGHTS ON

I was in my second year of Bible College, coming home late one night from a revival church service. I was driving a Toyota Celica, my favorite car, and I was excited at all that God was doing. I was in the midst of one of the greatest revivals, long awaited, hoped for and needed. This was a revival of the church, the people of God.

While driving home, I pulled up to the first stop light, and the car next to me honked its horn. I turned and smiled as the person waved at me. I remember thinking, wow, it is so cool to see all that God is doing and to be surrounded by people being touched by God.

Then as I continued home, another car began honking at me, and I remember waving at first, and then getting frustrated when they persisted. All the way home, cars continued to honk at me, trying to wave me over, like I had done something wrong.

As funny as it sounds, I was really getting angry. Here I was having a God moment and all these people were trying to take it away. If only they knew me, if only they knew what was going on inside the car, then maybe they could have a little grace and mercy and leave me alone for just one second. But no,

Taking Back the Night

every light, every car that passed by honked, gestured, waved. And all the way home, I became more and more frustrated and angry.

Until...

Pulling into my driveway, I finally realized what everyone else knew and I was too dense to understand. As my car pulled up towards the garage I noticed my headlights were not reflecting off the closed garage door like they normally did.

> **INSTEAD OF INFECTING THE WORLD FOR CHRIST, WE END UP BECOMING INEFFECTIVE**

My lights had gone out.

I had turned them on, but the bulbs had burnt out. The power was gone.

This is what happens when Christians get behind the wheel of a vehicle, whether it's religion, a program or a Sunday morning service. They start it up, they have songs and music, they preach the word, they have their potlucks. The vehicle is there; they take it for a drive around and say, look at my nice, new car. But the whole time it is not reflecting Christ; the whole time it has no power.

A vehicle that drives in the night but does not shine any light is dangerous. It is in jeopardy of crashing or, more importantly, hitting an innocent bystander. One of the most dangerous things that has happened in the church's struggle to stay alive, to avoid change, is that it has taken many down with it. There is a whole generation that despises us for trying to force them into a mold that Christ never intended. Just like the Jewish believers in the New Testament who demanded that the Gentiles become circumcised, we have forced a generation

Driving With The Lights On

to fit our expectation of Christianity instead of letting them encounter God on His terms. So instead of infecting the world for Christ, we end up becoming ineffective.

Jesus says that we are the light of the world; we are a city on a hill. We are the salt, and if the salt loses its saltiness then it is of no use. Throw it out.

Who is the light? Who is the salt? The church! Jesus continually challenges His disciples, the church, to stay effective in this world. Yet the church constantly looks at the world and says, why aren't you changing? And, if you won't change then you are of no use to God; we must throw you out.

Christ never talks about throwing the world away. He talks about how a light must shine, and about salt that loses its saltiness being no good for anything, but He doesn't talk about throwing the world away.

Now I know that there is a day coming when God will judge the nations. Sinners will be judged, but so will Christians. The sad part is that, once we get saved, we can forget that we are still being held accountable for our actions, or lack thereof. Salvation isn't the free pass to live life how you want to, now that you have eternal life. In fact it's really a free pass to truly die to your self. The point is, God will judge those who ultimately refuse His gift, His sacrifice, but until that day comes, we are required to do all that we can to save them.

- 4 -

BEING SALTY

When I was in Bible College, many people were surprised that I was from California. They would say that California was going to drop off into the ocean; one more big earthquake and we were all gone.

After hearing this over and over again, I finally stopped one man who was talking about how San Francisco should be ready for the next big one. Even now I cannot believe the absurdity of some of the conversations I engaged in. I would have to stop and say, how can you even be thinking this; have I just stepped into the twilight zone?

So I asked him, why do you think this, why do you think the next earthquake is going to drop San Francisco like a bad habit? His response: God must judge the city for its sins.

I couldn't believe it. What about the fact that Christ died on the cross for their sins? His immediate response was, they have blasphemed the Spirit by ignoring His pleas and therefore must be punished. He said that San Francisco makes Sodom and Gomorrah look like Disneyland. I thought that was the last straw, but he followed it up with, if God doesn't punish San Francisco he will have to apologize to Sodom and Gomorrah.

Taking Back the Night

I had a response, but to this day I do not believe that it made any difference. I used to love arguing the things of God. I thought that was what Christ would have wanted. I had my verses memorized; I loved debating the Bible. Simple things like, can Christians drink? Can a Christian be demon possessed? Are tongues or healing for today? Then one day God showed me, arguing is pointless, just show them My power. He said, fall more in love with Me, become intoxicated by Me and show them My power. Easy enough.

My arguing has never won anybody for the kingdom, but a true expression of Christ's power wins every time. A man with an argument can never win against a man with an experience. I have talked to people over and over again who say God doesn't heal today, and I used to argue with them till I was blue in the face, to no effect mind you. And then God told me, stop arguing about whether I heal or not and let's just start getting some people healed.

The person who has an argument that God does not raise people from the dead today will have a hard time convincing the person who was just raised from the dead. They are standing there, alive. No matter what you say, God did a miracle. And in a choice between having a powerful God who does miracles and heals, or having a powerless God, I am sure the formerly dead person would like to stay with the God of miracles, miracles for today.

I have also found that, despite their arguments, the moment they become sick, most people like having a God that heals. Why wait? I don't want to wait until the devil attacks before I start fighting the battle. I want to be a Christian on the offensive, already engaged in spiritual warfare. I want to send the gates of hell a notice that I am coming and Christ is coming with me.

Being Salty

So I now know that arguing with this guy in Bible College was fruitless, but what about Sodom and Gomorrah? What about this evil city filled with every kind of debased and vile sin? What was God's viewpoint and His desire for this city?

What God showed me amazed me. First let's set the picture. Abraham and his nephew Lot are living not too far from each other. They are finding it cramped, and so Lot takes the rich land of Jordan and pitches his tents near Sodom, while Abraham chooses the land of Canaan where God meets with him. Here God makes the first covenant with Abraham: I will be your God and you will be my people.

So Abraham has these God encounters, where God is literally coming down in the flesh and meeting with Abraham. Abraham is encountering a real God – powerful, passionate and intimate. In the midst of this great personal encounter, God

> I DON'T WANT TO WAIT UNTIL THE DEVIL ATTACKS BEFORE I START FIGHTING THE BATTLE

mentions that the cries of the sins of Sodom are so great that He will have to destroy this nation.

As a side note, in those intimate times with God some of His greatest secrets are revealed. It may be because we have finally shut up and let God speak. It may be because we are so close to the heart of God that we hear its every beat. Or it may be that God understands that intimacy requires becoming vulnerable, and it is at that moment that God reveals some of His greatest secrets.

Either way, that was where Abraham was, a place of pure

Taking Back the Night

intimacy with God, and God reveals to him that He may judge this sinful land. Those revelations can also be a character-building test from God. Here Abraham has a choice. How would he respond? He can agree with God – destroy the nation. He can go down into the city and proclaim God's judgment. Or He can intercede on the land's behalf. In this time of intimacy, God is asking Abraham, what are you going to do, what are you made of, what kind of man of God are you?

To those who walk in great prophetic anointing and to those who are just starting out, let me take a moment to interject something. When God reveals something to you, especially in the way of judgment, it may not be for you to proclaim so that they can see the mighty hand of God as He judges. Most likely, it is a test to see how you respond.

> WE FORGET THAT WE HAVE THE POWER OF CHRIST'S RESURRECTION INSIDE OF US

The closer you get to God, the more He begins to reveal His secrets, and He starts out slow, to see your character. He wants to know what you are going to do with it and how much maturity you have in the process.

I have been in church services when in the middle of worship someone will approach me and say, God has given me a word for the people. I will let them share the word with me, and then I send them back to their seat. A moment will pass, and they will come up again, God has given me this word and I need to share it, they say. I will let them know that I think we are okay, and send them back to their seats, where they sit and brew until they can handle it no more and walk out of the service, angry,

Being Salty

hurt and bitter.

One such person met with me later and asked why I didn't do anything about the word that God had given her? This was a word from God Almighty and I ignored it, how dare I? But my response got her attention.

First, I pointed out that the worship leader was addressing the very thing she'd just shared with me. I let her in on a little secret: she was not the only one who heard from God. God created spiritual authority and leadership, and He usually tries that route first. Just because you get a word from God does not mean you get to negate all the others that are written down in His book, the Bible.

I also let her know that God was curious about what she was going to do with the word He just gave her. She was okay in sharing it with me, but then when she was sent back to her chair, she should have begun praying, praying the heart of God, which is one of the most powerful tools we have as Christians, even though some of us think our most powerful tool is our mouth. Instead, not only did she not pray the heart of God, she gave way to the enemy and let him take away a God moment while she sat and stewed. She had an encounter with God, and it ended with an encounter with the enemy.

I have found that sometimes God just likes to reveal stuff to us because He can. He whispers softly just to know if we are listening, to draw us closer, to become intimate. It is not a status symbol or a revelation of our greatness; it is an opportunity to become closer with Christ, to encounter Him.

Abraham's Choice

Abraham has an encounter with God, and God reveals something to him, as a test of his character – I am going to

Taking Back the Night

destroy Sodom and Gomorrah. Abraham could have run down and warned everyone: the judgment of God is coming, prepare yourselves. But Abraham realized that he had right in front of him the one who controlled their destiny. He had an opportunity to move the heart of God, and not only to move it, but to pray the heart of God.

So Abraham responds, surely you will not destroy the righteous with the unrighteous? Abraham begins to intercede on behalf of the people. What is intercession? Simply praying the heart of God.

I do not believe that God truly desired to destroy Sodom and Gomorrah; I believe that God's heart was to save them.

So then the angels of the Lord visit Sodom and stay with Lot. This is where it becomes truly interesting for me. Everyone always bad-mouths Lot for living in Sodom. If you pitch your tent near Sodom, don't be surprised when you fall into sin, they say. I have heard that message preached far too many times, and as far as I can see, all it has done is keep us from interacting with the very ones Christ interacted with, the sinners.

In fear of falling into any sin, we avoid the sinful at all cost. When the truth is, sinners are going to sin. When we believe that the power in this world is greater than the God in us, we have lost sight of the power of Christ. We are so worried about the power of the enemy, the power of sin, the power of temptation that we forget that we have the power of Christ's resurrection inside of us. Greater is He in us! We can overcome, not by staying away from sin, but by the blood of the Lamb, the word of our testimony, and by not loving our life, even if it means we die.

We must get to a place where we are not so concerned with living. This world is not that great when compared to what God

Being Salty

has for us. Therefore let me pitch my tent near Sodom. I am not afraid of what the devil brings to my door because I know who lives with me and I shall overcome.

Of course, if you have an issue with alcohol, please do not pitch your tent near a bar. If you have an issue with sex, do not visit the brothels and base your ministry there. However, please do not use the fact that you once were a sinner as a reason to never interact with them again. Paul had been the greatest of sinners, which made him of great effect for the kingdom of God.

Sodom needed God, and who was going to bring Him to them? Sodom needed righteousness, but who was going to take it? Sodom needed a real, manifest presence of the power of God, and if not Lot, then who? We are always expecting God to move, but we don't want to have to move ourselves.

I remember in High School, I was always praying, God let your Spirit fall. Right here in the lunch room, let your revival fire fall, just like it was with Elijah. I would tell God that if He sent His Spirit down in power, then I would jump up on the table and start preaching. Or, if His conviction would hit them in the school room and grip their hearts to the point they were weeping at their desks, then I would start telling them boldly about the goodness of God.

The problem therein lies with me. God loves using people. He could do it, I have no doubt, but He longs to use us. He longs for us to desire His heart and to take the steps to achieve His destiny for others. He says, you jump up on that table and start preaching and then my fire will fall. You start sharing Christ with others and then I will start gripping their hearts. Faith usually requires action first.

Sodom needed God. San Francisco needs God. Not more

Taking Back the Night

judgment; it has plenty of that. It needs love. What it really needs is Christians who come not only in word, but also in power.

So Lot is living in Sodom, and his problems are too numerous to even count. He has negotiated with sin. He is clearly keeping a foot in both worlds. He knows God when he sees Him, yet he wants to appease the world when it comes knocking at his door. The men of God come to Sodom, and Lot recognizes them. He invites them into His house.

The problem wasn't Lot living in Sodom; the problem was Sodom living in Lot

This is such a representation of Christians who accept Christ into their hearts, and then at the first temptation of sin negotiate with it. The men of the town want to molest the men in the house, so what does Lot do? Instead of saying, this is God in my house; do you know who you are messing with? He appeases the men by saying they can have relations with his daughters.

Lot's compromise with sin comes to a head later, when the daughters have incestuous sin with their father. The sins of the father reaped by their children. It doesn't have to be that way, but Lot never sets the record straight. He never calls down righteousness. Lot is oblivious to his compromise. The problem wasn't Lot living in Sodom; the problem was Sodom living in Lot.

So, what happens when salt loses it saltiness? Lot was supposed to be infecting Sodom with the presence of God; instead, he

Being Salty

compromised with the world and was no longer of any effect.

With this man I spoke with in Bible College, his view of San Francisco grieved me because the cries of the sins had surpassed the cries of the people of God praying the heart of God. Instead they were praying for it to just go away, to fall off into the ocean.

God wanted to spare Sodom, but he needed someone to stand in the gap. I find what happens next in the story ironic. When Lot's wife looked back, I believe it was with a measure of remorse, wondering, could she have saved it? And with a measure of sorrow, wondering, would she ever have it again? She had a desire to save Sodom and a desire to enjoy sin. Her foot in both worlds, she is turned into a pillar of salt, the very thing that she was supposed to be the whole time she lived there. She was supposed to be affecting that world for God, so ultimately she became what she was supposed to be, salt.

So what I wish I had told this guy back in Bible College was simply this: instead of giving up on it, why don't you go do something about it? Try being salt; that is what God made you.

There is a generation out there right now that many consider a Sodom and Gomorrah generation. They are growing up believing that homosexuality is okay, something you are born with. They grow up believing that premarital sex is the norm. They believe that relationships do not require sacrifice, but rotation. This generation needs some that are willing to pitch their tents in the heart of the darkness and demand that the light shine.

I do know that there will be a day when every nation will be judged and will pay for its sins, but until that day I am going to try and steal as many souls into the kingdom of God as I

TAKING BACK THE NIGHT

possibly can. I do not discount anyone. I will not give up on anyone. I am taking back what was rightfully ours to begin with. I am taking back the night.

PART 2
VENTURING INTO THE NIGHT

The unknown is the platform for destiny,
the stage in which living can commence.

- 5 -

ENTERING UNCHARTED WATERS

I received a prophetic word once that changed my life. The word itself was not that unusual, but that one word changed my perception on how I would receive and look at prophetic words from then on. The word was this, "I see you in a boat, in the water. It is a dark area of water and you are out on the edge. It is a part of water that no one has ever journeyed into before. And you have cast out your nets, all around you. And before you even begin pulling your nets in, the fish start jumping into your boat. Loads of fish, all sizes, all types. And your nets are full of fish. This will be the beginning of a great harvest."

When that word was given, it was during a service, in a room full of people, with me at the front. I heard the oohs and the aahs, the amazement of it all. I was going to be a part of a new harvest, a great harvest. Who would not want that? I just didn't truly understand the word.

Let me retell what was said from a different perspective. *You are going to be out in the water on a boat, in the dark water where no one has ever gone before.* So, I am going to be all alone, in this dark part of the water. I am going to be going against trends and traditions, against the flow, by going where no one

Taking Back the Night

has ever ventured before. That means, not everyone is going to like what I am doing. There is a reason no one has gone there before.

I am throwing out nets, by myself? Lots of work, and then *all these fish are jumping into the boat.* Hurray! Except I have never heard of a fish jumping into a boat already cleaned and gutted. That means for every fish that comes in, there is a cleaning process that needs to take place. When I look back at that word, I just shake my head. I had no idea what was in store.

I had been a children's pastor for five years at my church, when I woke up one morning and God told me it was time for a change. For my sake, it was time for a change. I truly believe that I was a good children's pastor; I loved children's ministry and I still do. I was trained by the best. But here I was five years in and God was calling me into the one area I never wanted to minister to – youth!

Now, let me explain, I was not called to be a youth pastor. I was called to pastor a generation. Not just a generation, but a movement, a revolution. I am a revolution pastor, if such a thing exists. I remember sitting down with my dad. Our youth pastor at the time was moving into a different area of ministry at the church, and a void was being left. They were having a hard time filling the gap.

So I shared with him the vision God had given me, the vision of a movement. I told him, I don't want to be a youth pastor, but I believe that God is going to use me to start a movement. Nations are going to be changed, a generation will be impacted.

That was great, but he didn't need a movement started, he needed a youth pastor, and if I left children's ministry, then he would need a children's pastor and a youth pastor. So for the moment, the answer was no.

Entering Uncharted Waters

I had walked into a conundrum. I truly believe in trusting the authority that God has given us. For me, that authority was my pastor, mentor, spiritual father and physical father. Yet, I had God telling me that He was calling me from children's ministry; that the grace would no longer be there. If you have ever worked in children's ministry then you know that it is hard enough *with* the grace there. If the grace was being taken, then I knew it was time to go. What to do, but pray?

Then two days before I was going to bring my resignation letter to my father, on a Sunday morning about two months after we had talked, I was sitting on the front row in our sanctuary when my mother asked, "Have you ever thought about youth ministry?" I looked her in the eyes and said, you need to talk to dad. My dad hadn't told her anything, but my mom had had a dream. God had showed her what was supposed to take place.

I was given one year. One year to work with the youth, while they continued to look for a real youth pastor, and then I would be out of a job. So I entered the arena of the unknown. I began my journey into these dark uncharted waters. Even as I write this, I know that there are those of you who have journeyed here as well. You are reaching some of the unreachable, in even greater, more unfathomable situations, and most likely in better, more powerful ways. What is so hard about reaching youth in a suburb of Sacramento, California?

That may be true, but I was messed up. I was not comfortable with just doing another youth ministry. There were two factors at play here – me and the calling. Much has been written about youth ministry, great concepts and ideas. When I took the office of 'youth pastor', I was given stacks upon stacks of teaching tapes and training books. *How to raise youth leaders, how to keep youth leaders once you have raised them, how to grow a*

Taking Back the Night

youth ministry, how to host a fun night. Books on games, quotes and sermon titles. And these are good resources – after all, who wants to reinvent the wheel? If you have an idea that works I'm happy to hear about it.

But I was battling with my own concepts; why do we do church anyway? I remember talking to my dad and saying that many of those coming to Club Retro would never set foot in our Sunday morning service. Many pastors would end that outreach right then and there. What is the point if they are never going to come to our church; how does that help us? That may be why many churches do not feed the poor; the poor are terrible tithers in their eyes.

Why would they not attend a Sunday morning church? Because they have no concept of that. Why sit around for a few hours and listen to someone speak and then go home? What is the point of that? I began to ask myself all of these questions.

> **WHEN I LET IN THIS NON—CHRISTIAN BAND, NON— CHRISTIANS CAME WITH THEM**

For what gain do we do youth ministry, children's ministry or any ministry for that matter?

We say, to enlarge the kingdom of God. Really?

How much of it is to simply please our attendees. Has church ministry become like the grocery wars that are being waged on every corner?

There was a time when you went to the grocery store because it was the only one in the area. No matter what they offered, you were grateful. Many of them were ma and pa operated.

Then someone with money came in and challenged the

Entering Uncharted Waters

locals by offering more items at a discounted price, putting the ma and pa stores out of businesses. Thus the Mega-Marts entered the picture.

But that wasn't enough; pricing wasn't the end of the story. We can choose baggers or no baggers, does your store have an in-house bank or just an ATM, is child care offered, will they walk you to your car, how quickly do they open up another lane during a rush? Is there a deli, pharmacy, coffee shop, fish counter and meat department? Then you can really get technical with organic and natural foods. The real question is, does it ever end?

Then there are the churches. More of them than grocery stores. I attended one church that sat on a road with over eight churches on it. Take your pick. We had home churches, mega churches, seeker-friendly churches. We had Pentecostal, Charismatic, Seventh-day Adventist, and Pentecostal/Charismatic home churches that met on Saturdays for the seeker crowd. Churches with choirs, without choirs, churches with seven services that included modern worship, blended worship, post modern worship, acoustic, a capella and everything else in between. To what end?

A seasoned pastor once told me, when I was preparing for the ministry, that if we didn't provide a cutting edge youth ministry, then the parents would go to a church that did. I thought, how tragic! My next questions were, who determines cutting edge and why do we care if the parents stay? His answers shaped the focus of my whole ministry for the next years. If the parents don't stay then we don't have a church; thus we don't have a pay check. Cutting edge is determined by the size of your youth group.

Ah ha, I thought. So God does not really play a part in it at

Taking Back the Night

all. Now it all makes sense. Before I had ever officially started ministry, I had figured it all out. I just didn't know it yet.

But now here I was in a special circumstance. I had been given the freedom of a year to see what God would do without having to meet some quota. I knew early on that we would not be the place for everyone. I have led many young people to the Lord who do not attend our church, and that is okay with me. Sometimes that is a better situation. I want people to go where they are going to grow, and when you lead a sixteen-year-old girl to the Lord and she says, now I am going to reconcile with my parents and go to their church, I am not touching that. The last thing she needs now is for some pastor to try to manipulate the situation to get another person filling their seats.

I also knew that some parents were not going to be okay with what we were bringing. Many expect the church to be a safe place for their child to attend. I'm okay with safe, but sterile, no! How effective would a maternity ward be if they could never make a mess? There would never be any children born, because child birth is messy. I know, I have three children.

So here I was. My problem was I didn't want to do what had been done before. I wanted to truly speak into the darkness and see the light shine. I remember walking through the halls of what was going to be Club Retro and looking at the flower-patterned wallpaper pasted to the walls and crying out to God. I wasn't a youth pastor, I didn't have clever ideas, but I was desperate to reach the lost and the dying.

For our first month, God told me that I was to do no preaching; I was just to make relationships with the young people. We held our youth services outside, due to the flower wallpaper inside, and we brought in Christian bands because we had no worship team. Desperation so often brings us to the

Entering Uncharted Waters

place where we begin to walk in obedience.

Then, one week it all changed. A young man in our youth group came to me and said that he was in a band that would love to play on a Wednesday night. The only problem was, they were not a Christian band; he was the only Christian in the band, the drummer. I said, why not? We looked over their lyrics and had them in.

Let me reveal my first secret, one that has been hidden from the church for a long time. When I let in this non-Christian band, non-Christians came with them. Yes, it is true. That night I had in front of me groups of unsaved young people. Most youth pastors would spend money to find a concept like this, and here a band comes knocking on my door wanting to play and brings the unsaved to me! These young people were not naïve. They had a preconceived idea of church and Christianity. We just burst that bubble for them.

- 6 -

GOD WANTS TO KILL YOU

I will confess; I have the most unpopular message in the world. I always joke that I wish I had Joel Osteen's message, "God loves you." Everyone likes that message. You write a book about how God loves you and the printers start rolling. You write a book about how God wants to bless you and people buy it by the truck load. You write a book about "God wants to kill you!" Not so popular!

I remember one night talking to some friends in the publishing industry. We were discussing a problem that a publisher was facing. This publisher had released a series of books by a well-known Christian author. The first book took the Christian world by storm. They could not keep it on the shelves. They followed it up with a version for children, one for women, a coloring book, a devotional, a book for men, an anklet, a key chain. Everything related that you could think of, they had it.

When the author decided to write a new book, the publisher wanted to be ahead of the game. So instead of waiting till after the book was published to make all the accessories, they made them in advance. The problem was, the first book was a 'bless me' book. The next book was one that required action from

Taking Back the Night

Christians. It did not do as well, and the publisher was finding themselves with lots of unwanted product.

God has called me to deliver a message that requires something from Christians – their life. That was my message that Wednesday night: God wants to kill you.

That was the first night I had felt released to share since beginning our Wednesday nights. The band was sitting right on the front row, watching their gear, surrounded by their unsaved friends.

> THAT WAS MY MESSAGE THAT WEDNESDAY NIGHT: GOD WANTS TO KILL YOU

I stepped up and said, there are two people who want to kill you, God and the devil. The devil wants to kill your soul and God wants to kill your flesh. Either way you are going to die. The question is, who kills you?

Not a popular message, but one that resonated in the young people that night. Salvations emerged. Transformations took place, and lives were changed.

There is a whole generation that is yearning to live for something worth dying for. We have that something. We have been walking around as if life was the most important thing, but in truth, when we die to ourselves we operate in a greater power. Yes, this generation is looking for zealots and extremists. They are looking for those who will not compromise with sin and who are real and transparent. Not perfect people, but broken people. And they do not want it to be based on a bunch of rules and regulations; they want it to be based on intimacy and a truly fanatical, passionate love of Abba Father.

God wants to kill you is an unconventional message, yet it is true. God is longing that we die to flesh. In this age of

God Wants To Kill You

extremists, of a generation that pushes everything to the limits, there is no reason to water down the message. They want it raw and they want it real. God loves you so much that He wants you to die. He wants you to lose your life, so that you can find it. Who says that? Jesus did, and it seemed to work for Him.

He was not simply trying to build a church. He had a kingdom mentality.

Jesus, in one day, performs many miracles, and many are following Him. Then in the next breath He turns to the crowd and says, you must eat my flesh to follow me. He doesn't give any explanation, He doesn't give a reason. He simply says, eat my flesh.

The crowd gets frustrated. They begin to murmur.

Jesus doesn't stop there. He says you must eat my flesh and drink my blood, again with no further explanation. The Bible says that after that, many turned away and followed Him no more (John 6:53-66).

The part that I think is interesting is that the disciples continued to follow him. Peter said, we have nothing left but you. Your words are life.

There is a generation that is willing to give it all up and live lives where the only thing they have is Christ. They are tired of a Christianity that tries to fit Christ into their lifestyle. They want a life that is based on Christ consuming everything. God, all I have is you.

THE WORLD COULD NOT STOP THEIR SINNING AND THE CHURCH IS NOT GOING TO STOP THEIR BELIEVING

Jesus was looking for the truly desperate. Those not only willing to leave it all to follow Him, but so desperate that they would stop at nothing. Those are the ones the church was built

Taking Back the Night

upon, and that is what Christ is still looking for today.

I love what Bill Johnson said once at a pastors' advance. He said, "If Jesus preached most of the sermons preached on Sundays in the average church, they never would have crucified Him." Why? Because we have watered down the message to keep people in the building, instead of getting them into the kingdom of God.

I love it when real evil sinners get saved. I am constantly surrounded by the best sinners and that is good ground for radical Christians. I love it when a Christian receives an encounter from God that causes them to start living a radical lifestyle, but when a non-Christian sinner gets saved from the dark, they go after the promises of God with reckless abandonment. They were extreme sinners and now they are extreme believers. The world could not stop their sinning and the church is not going to stop their believing.

We have all heard those people who come up to the newly saved and mumble under their breath, "One day the passion will die down and you will see what it is all about. One day you will be like me."

NO! I remember when I first came on staff in Sacramento someone told me that one day I would calm down, one day I would see that it is not worth all I was putting into it. I remember looking at them and saying, No Way! I don't ever want to be like that, I don't ever want to lose faith or hope. They corrected themselves and said that it would just be my stamina that would die down. My response was, then God would just have to rise up. Right now I pray for twenty people and two get healed. If my stamina dies down and I can only pray for ten people, then I expect to see all ten get healed. I guess my batting average would just have to increase with the supernatural of God, but don't you ever pull me down because you have become a lazy Christian.

So we began to change our youth services. We started bringing in unsaved bands and with them came the unsaved youth of a lost generation. We started to see powerful transformations, healings and encounters take place. We broke out of the mold of church and began to operate in power.

- 7 -

PRESSING IN FOR POWER

Call it the fast food culture. Call it a selfish nation, a people bred on the concept that all is theirs now, the microwave generation. Then change it. That is what church has been trying to do for years.

I have heard it said over and over again. We must change the mentality of this generation. They want everything now. I once heard a sermon entitled, 'Have it Your Way, a Burger King Lifestyle'. The preacher went on to give a sermon about having it your way or God's way. A Burger King lifestyle or a King of Kings lifestyle. It was clever, it was witty, and I bought into it.

We are constantly trying to change the world's mentality. Store up treasures in Heaven, run the good race in order to win the prize, anything to get them to desire something later that we cannot produce now.

Like dangling a carrot in front of a rabbit, or the proverbial wheel that we place the hamster in, we expect these young ones to continue running without ever receiving the prize, until they die of course. And then we wonder why our programs are not working, or why our God is not good enough.

Instead of trying to change their mentality, let us first look

Taking Back the Night

and see if it is even what God wants us to do!

I personally believe that we have a 'now' God, and the only reason we changed His way of doing things is that we could no longer provide the goods. Somewhere along the way we stopped experiencing the power of God, and in response we made up reasons why God no longer moves.

I remember one day, while I was in Brownsville during the Pensacola Revival, we received a call in the children's department. A man was bringing his stillborn child to the church to be prayed for. They couldn't get hold of the Senior Pastor yet and they wanted someone from the children's department to meet the man and begin praying for their child.

That day is vividly burned into my memory. I was stunned and excited. I went into the sanctuary with the children's pastor and a few of the other workers. The father brought his young child into the church's sanctuary in a portable styrofoam cooler. We all began to pray.

I was determined to see this child raised and life breathed into it. When they handed the child to me, I was shocked by how cold it was. In my arms was this potential for such destiny, taken, gone. I began to weep, to cry out. God, have your way, bring this child back. I knew His promises; I knew His desire. I knew that He was a good God. Yet, in the end, we all left that building without the miracle we longed for.

As we left, one of the workers placed his hand on my shoulder and said, "Matt, not everyone Jesus prayed for was healed." Then he walked away.

What? I was shocked. What kind of thinking is that? Firstly, it's not true. Jesus didn't pray for everyone, but everyone He prayed for was healed. Second, why is it in our human nature to excuse things away so easily? I didn't want an excuse; I wanted

Pressing In For Power

a God of power. That is what I had, and that is what I wanted.

For days, I locked myself in my room and cried out to God. I wasn't happy with the answer that sometimes God just does not heal. True, I have prayed for many since that day that have not been healed, but that does not cause me to expect any less. I don't understand it, and I know that I don't like it. I hate sickness and I hate disease and I will not settle for anything less than the truth that my God hates them as well. He has already paid the price for them, so I expect complete healing when I pray, because that is the promise I have.

We have revealed promises to this generation, and then tried to create excuses why they cannot have them. I can picture the day when the glory stopped falling as easily as it did the day before.

That day God was saying, just press in a little deeper. Cry out a little longer, desire a little more. How badly do you want it? One of the most frustrating revelations that God has given me was that He can tell your desire by the determination you put into it.

> **HE CAN TELL YOUR DESIRE BY THE DETERMINATION YOU PUT INTO IT**

I have Christians all the time who tell me, "You can't judge me." It's normally the Christians who want to get away with doing nothing for the kingdom that requires everything of them. The reality is, God can see the desires of the heart by the determination you put into your pursuit. I have people say, "I am just not outspoken," or "I am not a loud person." Personality has nothing to do with pursuit and determination. I have seen some of the quietest people, who when they want something, I would not dare stand in front of, because they are going to get

Taking Back the Night

it. I believe that God wants to know that we want Him.

I can see that day when the glory stopped. There had been healings, salvations, the moving of the Spirit. Then one day someone came up for healing and it didn't happen right away. One day, they tried to pray for the dead to be raised, and nothing happened. Then what? They could have pushed in, but instead they stopped.

Then they had to create reasons why God was no longer moving. They had promises that were not being fulfilled, and it couldn't be God's fault, so then it must be ours.

Why have we so easily been bought off by the lies of the enemy? They are not even good lies.

We have settled for lies like, it's a lack of faith, or it was not God's will, or they have sin in their life. What are we talking about?

I have heard people say that God did not heal because there was a lack of faith, either in the person praying or the person being prayed for. That is not even Biblical. Jesus said that if you have faith the size of a mustard seed then you can move mountains. Why a mustard seed? I can just see Jesus, frustrated with His disciples. They didn't see the results they wanted to see, and they think that there is some kind of formula. So Jesus has to explain to them. He's looking around for the smallest thing possible, and then He sees this little mustard seed and grabs it.

He holds this little seed in front of His disciples and He says, "See this – see how small this is? See how tiny this is? That is how much faith, how much formula, you need to see people get healed." Why? Because Jesus was saying, "It is not you; it is Me that does the healing!" If mustard seed size faith can move mountains, then it does not take much to see healings

Pressing In For Power

happen or the dead raised.

Yet, we persist in using it as a reason why people do not get healed. How much faith does a dead person have? Lack of faith cannot be a reason, because we have a God who longs to heal. By simply stretching out our hand and being willing, we are activating faith.

Then I hear people say that it is not God's will. That is wild nonsense. God hates sickness, He hates disease, and He has promised healing. Instead of making excuses why God doesn't heal and raise the dead, why don't we start petitioning the throne with His promises. Let's lay hold of the heavens and not let go till they come down.

I have found that I love putting God in awkward situations. I will be in the middle of a grocery store and see someone walking with a cane or on crutches, and I will feel the presence of God and go and pray for them and completely believe that God is going to heal them. I remember praying for one person who was not saved, and boldly telling them, God is going to heal you as a sign of His greatness.

Now, who is on the spot, me or God? I am just a vessel; I cannot heal anyone. I just create the opportunity for God to show His greatness. I say, God, now You do Your thing, because if You don't Your name is on the line.

God loves that. He loves it when His people begin to put a demand on His presence and do not settle for anything less.

We had a young man who got saved in Club Retro and it really stirred me, not simply because he got saved, but because Club Retro was all the church he would ever know. He never really came to Youth, or Young Adults, what many would classify as a real service. The only Sunday morning he came to was the one where he was baptized. And his salvation was a

Taking Back the Night

huge victory for our group. This young man, William, came to shows and was a part of Club Retro for a long time, and a group of our young men had prayed and fasted for months to see him get saved. So you can imagine the celebration we had when he accepted Jesus.

But William had a disease, and was slowly dying. After he was saved, we found out about his sickness and began to pray. Over the next few months William went from a healthy young man, to sickly, then deathly and in the hospital. Then one day we get the call that William had passed away.

I remember one of our leaders, Steve, was in a back room of Club Retro with some other guys, from a local Christian band. When they heard that William had passed, one of the guys stood in the room and said, "We should all pray."

Steve looked at them and asked why? "Well," said one of the guys, "We need to pray for William." Steve shot back, "Why would we pray for William, he has already passed away and none of you believe that God still raises people from the dead."

"Well, then let's pray for us. Let's pray that God comforts us in this loss," said one of the guys.

"No," said Steve. "I have been comfortable for too long. I think it is time I became uncomfortable."

I believe that is the resounding cry of this generation. They are tired of being comfortable. They just want to see a God that is true and real and powerful and madly in love with them.

We have a church in our area that has just spent massive amounts of money on top-of-the-line lighting and stage décor. In fact, during Christmas time they have actual snow that falls throughout the audience. None of that bothers me, and in fact I think it is kind of cool, but when the presence of God shows up and is real, it doesn't matter if you have state of the art sound

Pressing In For Power

or no sound system at all, you cannot keep people away. There is a generation that is longing for us to spend less time on the ambience and more time on getting the Spirit. They are tired of being comfortable.

That is my cry – God don't make me comfortable, make me passionate, desirous, ruined.

- 8 -

PERPETUATING INSANITY

Albert Einstein is often reported to have said that one definition of insanity is doing the same thing over and over again and expecting different results. According to this definition, many Christians have become insane. We keep operating in function over and over again, producing religion, but desiring outpouring.

In America we have a major problem. 82% say they are Christians, yet we have an increase in homosexuality, premarital sex, divorce, violent crimes, murders, and domestic abuse. And we wonder why the church is not making an impact on this world? If that is Christianity, then you can have it. That is what so many of this generation are saying.

One day, our church was doing a fireworks booth. We were passing out flyers to local homes and people in the community. An older man came up to our booth holding a flyer in his hand and not too happy about it. He told me that he was a Christian too, and that they had a booth a few blocks away from ours and that it was not okay for us to hand out flyers. He said that we were destroying the work of God by having young people handing out flyers. The amount of bitterness and anger in the man astounded me. Here he was representing Christ, but

Taking Back the Night

consumed by anger towards this generation.

I didn't understand him then and I don't understand him now. I looked at the guy and said I would make a deal with him. Our young people would stop handing out flyers if he stopped telling people he was a Christian. Because if he is Christianity and I am Christianity, then something is wrong. If 82% say they are Christians in America, someone somewhere is getting it way wrong. I don't want to be lumped into the mass of what everyone else is. God has called us peculiar and different, and that is what I want to be.

We were not called to be like the world but set apart. That is not defined by how we look, but by the presence of God.

One night in Club Retro I was called into our Spiritual Reading room. This is a room where our youth and young adults give prophetic words over those who come to the Club Retro shows. We have seen amazing healings, salvations and deliverances in these rooms, the power of God showing up.

But usually, when I am called into the room it is not when the presence of God is moving. In fact, I knew immediately what I would be facing. I tell my staff that whenever this happens to get me right away, because it is tough. When I arrived at the room I knew what I was dealing with – religious Christians. You could sense the spirit; it was stale, harsh and bitter.

Three young people, two girls and a young man, sat in the chairs opposite my team. I entered the room and asked how I could help. Instantly the young man wanted to argue with me about whether God heals today or not. As you read earlier, I no longer like to argue. I thanked the three and asked them to leave the prophetic room.

The young man persisted. He opened his Bible, conveniently brought with him, and began to spout scriptures at me. And

Perpetuating Insanity

again, I said that we were not going to argue and asked them to leave the room.

The young man was getting angry. "What kind of Pastor are you?" he asked me. With that, I stopped and looked at him. I wanted him to hear a few things. First, I told him, I am not a pastor but a leader of a revolution. Secondly, I told them all, their salvation was secure. They had their pass to Heaven and eternal life.

Yet, while sitting in these seats, longing to argue with me, they were taking an opportunity from someone else who might not know God and wanted to experience Him. Thirdly, if I brought someone in that room dying from cancer and asked them to choose one person to pray over them, who did he think they would choose? Would it be him, who did not believe that God heals, but would comfort them in their death, or me, who believes that God would heal them completely, and restore them?

With that, the young man got angry, stood up and began shouting at me. It was then I had to get our security in to escort these Christians off our property. When I went out of the room I saw one of my friends playing an arcade game. This guy is a radio host on one of the top rock stations in our area. I stood next to him as he played and he turned towards me and said, "Matt, I have been to churches before and I like your Jesus best." With that he turned back to his game and kept on playing.

Not long after that, my talk show friend brought his deaf daughter to the Club to be prayed for. Why? Because he saw something real and he wanted to experience more.

I tell people all the time, they might have experienced Jesus, but they might not have experienced my Jesus. Because my God is a powerful God, a healing God, a God who longs

Taking Back the Night

to transform the world around you. My God is real, and He is longing to invade the church once more.

- 9 -

THE MOST POWERFUL WEAPON

Why do we do the things we do? Why church on Sunday morning? Why church in a building? Why prayer meetings? Why rallies?

I believe we tried to regulate Christianity in America instead of impacting darkness with who God is.

I have struggled with a period of time that we Christians went through. I call it the prayer movement. Hundreds of thousands across the country gathered together to pray. We came to rallies, crusades, prayer nights, prayer meetings. Events started up like IHOP, BURN, 24-hour prayer meetings. All of them have the potential to be great, yet I was not satisfied.

I remember waking up one morning and asking God why I was having odd feelings about prayer. How can I not love this idea, a generation coming together and praying, crying out for the heart of God to be moved?

God's answer stirred me: we are the answer to the very prayer we are praying. What did He mean?

One of my spiritual fathers Martin Scott shed light on this one evening for me. He said that we have cleared the spiritual landscape. We have torn down the high places in the Spirit, yet we have failed to occupy.

Taking Back the Night

He used the scripture in Matthew 12:43-45, where Jesus says if a demon is sent out of a person but the person is not filled with God, then seven more will come back, fiercer, more intense, and more destructive. He said this is what we have done. We drove the demons out, yet we have not occupied the land, so we have created a place were the enemy has come back in, stronger, bolder, with greater numbers, and reoccupied.

Finally, it began to make sense to me. My problem is not with prayer. Prayer is vital, important. I have grounded my ministry on the concept that you cannot have breakthrough if you have not prayed through. You must lay the ground work in the spiritual before you can see the breakthrough in the physical.

But we have prayed, and ended with that. We hold the rallies; we have the 24-hour prayer nights. Yet we have failed to occupy the land. Prayer without putting it into practice is falsehood.

> God's answer stirred me: we are the answer to the very prayer we are praying

In Sacramento, it was frustrating to see hundreds of people come together every week for a prayer house, yet I had hundreds of unsaved coming to Club Retro and I was begging for help. Their prayers were getting answered, the unsaved were coming, yet they didn't want to fulfill the other part of the equation – seek and save the lost.

I had a conversation with a young man who was part of one of these prayer movements. He was greatly offended at my revelations. He began to cite Scripture on the importance of the prayer houses, and what was first established in Levitical law,

The Most Powerful Weapon

what was created with King David and the importance of what Jesus did when He went away to pray.

I agreed, meeting with God and praying is awesome, vital, a foundation. Let's just not negate the most important thing that came as a command from Jesus' own lips, "GO!" Go into all the world and preach the good news.

Jesus did not say some stay and some go. He said GO! Why do we spend so much time trying to link pieces of Scripture together to validate our ministries instead of just laying hold of simple commands of God and doing them with excellence?

For so long the church of America has done the same thing over and over again expecting different results. How about this? Let's simply do what God has asked of us and then see the results that have been promised.

I talked with another young girl who was telling me about a prayer meeting and demonstration they were having over an abortion clinic.

She said that they would be praying all night for this clinic to be shut down. So I asked her what kind of results they had seen. She told me that they had prayed for weeks for one clinic to be shut down, and then one day a sign was on the door saying the clinic was closed. It ended up being closed for three days. She rejoiced and praised God for the babies that were spared. Praise God, we know that there is power in prayer, why does that amaze us so much?

But I asked her, what did you do in those three days? I remember her looking at me puzzled. What do you mean, what did we do in those three days? We began praying over another clinic, she said.

Wow, how lost we have become. I remember telling this girl that the end of abortion would not come from prayer alone,

Taking Back the Night

to her shock. Is prayer important? Yes, absolutely vital. But I don't have to pray for the answer for girls who are considering abortion; I am the answer. The point is this, we are the salt of the earth, we are the light – we are supposed to shine.

In those three days, we could have met the girls coming, and prayed with them for strength. We could have talked to them about adoption, helped them with making good choices. We could have connected them to Jesus, and allowed His glory to fill their lives. Instead we did nothing, but rejoiced in a closed building.

Let's not forget, sinners are going to sin. Why does that still surprise people? What we need to do is connect people to Christ and let Him invade their lives. He is the answer that they are looking for, and we are the deliverer of that package.

So should we pray for clinics to be closed? YES YES YES! Should we stop there...? NO! We are not even beginning to scratch the surface of what God has called us to do if we pray without occupying.

PART 3
BRINGING AN ENCOUNTER

No one can stop the sun on its flight,
once it's awakened it is the end to night.

- 10 -

AN INCONVENIENT TRUTH

One day, one of my leaders was driving by a school in our area. There was a group across the street holding signs that said, "Homosexuality is a sin!", "AIDS will kill you!" They were wearing t-shirts with slogans like, "I will not keep silent!" and "Homo's go to hell!"

What is wild is that all of these statements hold elements of truth. AIDS will kill you. Homosexuality is a sin. These are truths; these are what I call convenient truths.

I do not believe our job as Christians is to simply state the obvious. Is that the level of our revelation from the throne room? Our prophetic prowess is in pointing out what others already know?

I can just imagine a person infected with the AIDS virus, oblivious to the direness of their situation. They walk past the Christian holding the sign saying, AIDS will kill you. They think, yes! Now they know they are going to die. They eagerly grab the hand of the person holding the sign, "Thank you for telling me AIDS is going to kill me. I didn't know. But now I do, thank you!"

That doesn't happen. Why? Because sinners don't need to be

Taking Back the Night

reminded that they are in sin, or distant from God; they know that. They can feel that. There is an emptiness, a groaning from the deep that is longing to be filled; that is what makes sharing the gospel so easy.

The person with AIDS knows what caused it; they know that it will kill them. The person holding the sign is telling them a truth, but that is not the truth Christ died on the cross to give. His truth is this: AIDS may kill you, but I have come to heal you!

That is the inconvenient truth. It requires that Christians learn to love a dying world and be willing to do something about it. The world does not need Christians standing across a street telling them that as sinners they are going to hell. The Pharisees did that; the Sadducees did that. What they need is for more of us to cross the street, grab them by the hand and let them encounter the supernatural, physical manifestation of the presence of God.

Why are these truths inconvenient? They require us to act. They require death to the flesh. They require light to shine. How do we impact darkness? By standing in the middle of the night and allowing Christ to shine through us. It is what John G. Lake did when he went to Africa and entered the middle of the hotbeds of sickness and gave them an encounter with the presence of God. It is what Mother Theresa did when she left the safety of her convent to walk the streets to love and encounter the poor and needy. It is what God has called you and me to do as well.

What we do so often is mistake compelling with convincing. We want to convince people into the kingdom, with clever words and catch phrases. God longs for us to compel people with a simple encounter with Him. When we stop operating in the

An Inconvenient Truth

presence of God, then we lose the ability to compel hearts; that is when we start trying to convince.

I have decided I am no longer going to convince someone to enter into a relationship with God. No one had to convince me to enter into a relationship with my wife. There was no one standing across the street holding a sign that said, Matthew, if you do not marry her then you are stupid. No, I fell in love with my wife. Her very presence in a room makes me weak at the knees. That is how my God works.

I get the amazing opportunity to introduce my Beloved to those who have never encountered Him before, and He is breathtaking. His very presence changes the atmosphere wherever He goes, and I bring Him with me always. I no longer have to convince; I simply introduce.

- 11 -

THE POWER OF AN ENCOUNTER

What does it take to impact a life so much that one would change the course of their life forever? A God encounter.

I have watched late night television and seen the accounts of those who claim to have had encounters of the third kind – visitations from another world, beings from other planets taking them off in the night. Those encounters, which were not even Godly – encounters of the mind, encounters with drugs, encounters with demonic forces – have changed people's lives forever.

How much more so with a God encounter?

I am often baffled by those who have had encounters with God that are true and powerful and then allow themselves to fall away from the supernatural.

There was a family in our church that God completely touched, and healed a serious health problem. The miracles they saw were so many you could not even count them. In the end, they left over frustrations with relationships and entered a fellowship that did not move in miracles. I still scratch my head and wonder, how can you do that? There is nothing that could take me away from moving in the supernatural of God.

Taking Back the Night

I don't care what you say about me or how you hurt me, I am not going to lessen my encounter with God because of you. God encounters are so much more than simply a physical manifestation; they are intimate and powerful.

When you operate out of function without an encounter, all you are left with is religion – dead, powerless religion.

I tell parents constantly, do not make your child go to my youth group or my church. Do I feel that as parents we can make our child go to church? Yes, and as long as my children live in my house they will go to church as well. But what church, and where, is a totally different subject. I want my child to go to church somewhere that they are going to encounter God, and that may not be where I encounter God.

Not all youth will encounter God deeply at our fellowship. Our worship is loud, our message can be challenging, and our concepts can be foreign. We may not be what everyone is looking for, or needing at the time. I want young people to go where they are going to encounter God, no matter where and how long that takes. Now, if you are reading this and still shaking your head, this is obviously not a book for you. I will take this as a time to point out why. There is common sense to throw out, and there is common sense to hold on to. Both are Biblical. The common sense to throw out is man's sense; we need to operate not in the mind of man, but with the mind of Christ (1 Cor. 2:16). The common sense to keep is the Godly sense that is now instilled in us. Love believes all things (1 Cor. 13:7), good things. So, obviously there is more to telling my child that they can go to whatever church they want.

Yet, if my child is encountering God at the church down the street, I am not going to force them into the old school way of

The Power Of An Encounter

thinking that they must go to all my events as well. I do believe that we are in competition, but not with the church down the street. The only competition I am in is this one: let's get people into the kingdom of Heaven. If you want to deal with them after that, go ahead; that gives me more time to go fishing – for souls!

We keep trying to work using old school thinking, with new trains of thought. What we need to do is put new wine in new wine skins.

I have had kids that go to our group, and then leave to attend the Baptist church down the street. I don't say, "Oh no! They have friends at the church down the street, they might leave my church." I have had parents who get worried: is Pastor Matt going to be hurt, will he notice they are gone, what do I do to get them back? I tell the parents, the worst thing you could do is force your child back to our church. The Baptists have a lot that we Pentecostals could learn. With that said, if we are burning bright then we should be affecting the church down the street, just as much as the world around us.

We have had numerous young people attend our group that also go to other youth groups. I talked to a young man one night, and found out that he was the worship leader for his youth group. He wanted to know if it was okay if he came here on Wednesdays to soak up some God before he went to his youth group on Fridays. I told him, no problem – come on in and encounter God. The next week he brought his whole worship team with him. Get God, and then bring Him back to where you are and set that place ablaze.

We have had whole groups of young people join our leadership team while they were still leaders of youth groups in other churches. Not because we were trying to steal them away, but because we had placed them to infect other Christians with

Taking Back the Night

the supernatural power of God. They were potential encounter beacons of the supernatural.

The Cost of an Encounter

I have found that the reality of an encounter often proves to be more difficult than I first thought. From the beginning of the Bible to the end, the people who have had God encounters can tell you – they change your life. A God encounter defines who you are.

We pray constantly for God encounters. We put them in clever little worship songs and we ask God daily for them. In our church, at what started as Thursday night meetings, our pastor would pray at the opening of every service, God come down and change me. Encounter me.

Did we even know what we were doing?

I do not believe I was ready for the encounter I was about to get. I know that God will not give me more than I can bear, and yet He also longs to give me the desires of my heart. I bore it just fine; I survived (in death), yet in the process of an encounter, God strips you to the core of who you truly are.

When I open the Bible, I am challenged by Abraham. What kind of God encounter did he have that caused him to take his whole family and begin to wander into the unknown? His simple act of obedience was the seed of a nation that would change the world. But his obedience was birthed from a God encounter.

His God encounter swept him up and captured his heart and moved him into something that lasted more than a moment – he believed. He believed that there was something greater than him, something greater than now, and he wanted to lay hold of it and invest in it.

The Power Of An Encounter

It is the same kind of God encounter that Moses had with a fiery bush, and Joshua had as he took off his sandals before the Angel of the Lord (Joshua 5:15). It is the same encounter that David had while he played his harp and before he led his armies. The same encounter that Job had in the midst of a great storm. The same encounter that Isaiah had producing a life-altering revelation. The same encounter every disciple had before they left all they knew to simply follow Jesus.

It is the same encounter that every single story in the Bible is based on, throughout the Old and New Testaments. Like Saul on the road to Damascus, or Peter when he declared Jesus was the Christ.

What did it take for a disciple to encounter Christ? He called them from a distance, "come follow me." Three little, life-changing words. To leave all that they had – family, jobs, and friends. To let the dead bury their own dead. In today's world, Christ's words might appear manipulative. People would say, do not put the calling before your family. Yet the disciples' obedience following an encounter helped create the foundation for the church.

One of the most frustrating encounters in the Bible to me is the story of the rich young ruler. His encounter defined his life.

In Matthew 19:16, you find the rich young ruler coming to Christ. He wants to know how to obtain eternal life. I could spend pages taking apart his encounter, but I want to get to the meat of this story.

THIS GENERATION PLACES VALUE ON THINGS BY THEIR COST

I have heard people say that his motivation to meet Christ

Taking Back the Night

was wrong; he just wanted eternal life. Yet, throughout the Bible you have accounts of those who seek God for personal gain, such as healing, and God meets them there, and their lives are changed.

I do not believe it was his motive that was wrong. What he wanted and what he needed were two different things, and he was not willing to pay the price for the latter. The rich young ruler encountered the giver of eternal life, yet he was not looking for an encounter, he was looking for a formula.

He had already professed to having obeyed all the commandments (Matthew 19:16-20). This is when Christ confronts him with the condition of his heart. The sacrifices of God are a broken and contrite heart, not function. God instantly hits the issue. He says, let's get real. You want to know what eternal life is; it is laying down this life.

> Jesus said to him, "If you want to be perfect, go, sell what you have and give to the poor, and you will have treasure in heaven; and come, follow Me."
>
> But when the young man heard that saying, he went away sorrowful, for he had great possessions. (Matthew 19:21-22)

His encounter defined him. It instantly ranked where God was in his life. So often our encounters with God draw a line. Every time we want to move closer to God, there are going to be greater levels of sacrifice required of us. Greater levels of death to the flesh.

What we don't realize is that there is a generation that has nothing left to live for. They are actually longing for someone to

The Power Of An Encounter

require something of them.

When we first opened the doors to Club Retro, we were determined to do free concerts. We were going to have free concerts with great bands, and open them up to everyone, and then we would preach during the concert, at some point. This seemed like a great idea. The gospel is free, the message is free, eternal life is free. So, free concerts should follow.

Now, God had already convicted me of trying to trick kids into the kingdom. The world is wise to our clever ways; they know when they are being duped into hearing a message.

I remember going to one youth event where they would lock the doors so no one could leave until after the message. They had huge bounce houses, sumo suites, skate ramps and you could use all the items; you just couldn't leave until after the message. It was the price you had to pay; you must listen to my message if you want to use my stuff. I don't believe we should work like that anymore.

If our message is so great, then we shouldn't have to lock kids in and force them to listen to it. I want to see people flocking to us because the power of God is drawing them in. If what we are offering is real, then we shouldn't need to trick kids into the kingdom. That is why God said we have power. Go, raise the dead, cast out demons, heal the sick, be examples of the presence of God. Before Christ would share, He would give a demonstration of power. Give this generation an encounter with something real.

We used to do free concerts with preaching, and they never worked. First, God asked me why I was preaching. He didn't need another preacher; He needed someone willing to shine. Then, when we would open the doors, we found that virtually

Taking Back the Night

no one would come.

I couldn't understand why. It frustrated me. Here we were doing free shows for the community, for the kids. Then it hit me. This generation places value on things by their cost. If it doesn't cost me anything, then it must not be that great. I would take the same exact shows that we were doing for free and slap a $10 charge to them and have a hundred kids show up.

I was putting a value to the shows. I was saying, this show is so great that it is worth $10. What we have done for so long with the gospel is say, it is so great that it is free. This gospel does not cost you a dime.

I had to repent from the frustration that I held towards the person that told me that eternal life was free. Eternal life is not free; it costs you everything. Your life is no longer your own. We have lied to generations because we want more people to fill our pews instead of filling the kingdom of Heaven. There is a generation of young people out there that see no value in Christianity, and we have done it to ourselves.

We need to restore the value of a life of Christian living. We restore the value by putting a price to it. Yes, I know, Christ paid the price for us. He paid the ultimate price, by dying on the cross. Yet, does that mean no one else may have to die on a cross? Look at Peter.

The ultimate price was paid, yet there is a price we all must pay. For some it will be easier, because we come to the table with nothing. For others, like the rich young ruler, he had much to lose, and for him the price was too great. Yet the value of the sacrifice is the same.

We have downgraded the encounter to a concept. I could teach the concepts of basketball all day. I could maybe fill a class or a workshop, but people do not fill stadiums for concepts; they

The Power Of An Encounter

fill stadiums to see a team play basketball. We are not going to fill the kingdom of Heaven by simply teaching concepts; we need to begin operating in the power that God has encountered us with.

That is why I encourage parents to allow their child to encounter God wherever they will encounter Him. Just make sure they encounter Him. I have seen too many fall away from God because their mind was filled with concepts but their spirit was void of an encounter. If I could have just one prayer, my prayer would be for the parents. Parents, please allow your child to encounter God. Spend as much time and energy setting your child up for an encounter as you do getting them on a football team.

> THE CHILDREN HAVE JUST ENOUGH TIME TO GET RELIGION BUT NOT ENOUGH TIME TO ENCOUNTER GOD

I have cried tears over the thought that parents will sit for hours with smiles on their faces watching their children practice in a sport that they may be awful at. They will arrange their schedules just to make sure their child gets to practice on time. They invite family and friends to watch them play a game. Yet when it comes to God, they will pull their child up off the altar during an encounter with God, when they are ready to leave.

Then we sit back and wonder why our children grow up and want nothing to do with God. It is because the children have just enough time to get religion but not enough time to encounter God.

Some might be thinking, God should move a little quicker. I guarantee the disciples in the upper room wished God would

Taking Back the Night

have moved a little quicker as well. Yet He waited. He waited until desperation translated into motivation, God's motivation.

God is looking for our level of desperation.

Encounters do not usually happen on our timetable, but on a Heavenly one. One where the fruits of the Spirit finally match up with the gifts.

- 12 -

DESPERATION MOVES THE HEART OF GOD

When we first started *Consecrated*, which originated as our worship group for the youth, God began to give me songs that I was afraid to sing – songs that you would not find in most churches. I remember the night God gave us one song that really challenged people.

We were sitting on a church platform. This church had invited me to come and speak to their congregation and asked *Consecrated* to play. It was about an hour before the service started, and we had locked the doors to the sanctuary, even locking out the pastor. I was at the keyboard in total frustration. I didn't want just another service. In truth, I didn't even want to be there, because I didn't feel I had anything to offer. I was tinkering on the keys and the other guys in the band were just praying around the room. They could tell I was just moments away from telling them to pack up because we were going to head home.

Then the Spirit of God came upon me, and as I was tinkering on the keys I began to sing, "I'm still waiting." It was one key, C#m – three notes, and a simple refrain, "I'm still waiting." And then my heart began to groan. I'm still waiting. The band moved to their instruments and a powerful song was birthed. That night the glory came down.

At the end of the service, a lady came to me and said, "What are you waiting for? Your song was all about waiting, what are you waiting for?" So I told her, I am waiting for God to be true to His word, to be faithful to His promises. She looked back at me shocked. "What kind of worship song is that?" she asked. Then she walked off.

It is the kind of worship song that moves the heart of God. I think God is waiting for His people to start longing for something real and to not be satisfied with what they have so far. There is so much more to be had, so much more to be tasted, so much more to be experienced. I am still waiting.

When I began to look in the Word, God gave me some wild revelation. We all love King David, and many worship leaders have put his songs into contemporary music, but I found that we are being selective about which of his songs we use today.

We have all heard the ones like, *as the deer panteth for the water so my soul longs after you.*

We love the songs that are sweet and uplifting, but how real are those for people who live real lives and have real issues, real circumstances and problems? What do they care about a deer panting for water if they cannot pay rent this month?

I remember sitting with one youth whose parents attended our church. He was struggling with salvation – what did it matter, was Christ real? He said one of his biggest frustrations was that his parents would come and dance around in the worship service and then go home and scream and yell. It was all just a game.

He was having a hard time worshipping God because he didn't want to dance around; he didn't have a reason to dance.

Desperation Moves The Heart Of God

He was struggling in life, struggling with family, struggling with issues, and what he wanted to do was come to the throne of God and scream and yell, but he was not given that chance. He was only allowed to sing and dance, and pant at the water.

When I looked at David, he did a lot of screaming and yelling, a lot of petitioning before the throne, a lot of crying and pleading with the heart of God, long before he started singing and dancing. Real heart-cry issues resulted in real encounters with God that produced reasons to sing and shout.

I have thrown off the falsehood of religion and the simple operation of function, and I have begun to move only out of passion and desire. I come before the throne with fanaticism and zeal, and I cry out to my King. It is there in that throne room that I am met and transformed.

- 13 -

SUPERNATURAL EXPECTANCY

When we encounter God out of duty, we can leave disappointed. When we encounter God out of desire and desperation, then we become transformed.

I once heard a preacher say that everyone who encountered Christ was changed for the good. As I have already stated, every encounter brings revelation to our condition, but we are not always changed for the better. The rich young ruler, it says, left sorrowful and disappointed. How is it possible to meet with the King of Kings and Lord of Lords and leave disappointed?

I was in the middle of a worship service when God asked me, "What cry propels you before the throne?" What cry, what issue has gripped my heart to such a level that it has consumed me? I become inundated by the urgings of my heart, and that desperation drives me to an encounter.

One of the greatest threats to the new church generation in America today is loss of expectancy. Perhaps they have experienced too much. Familiarity breeds contempt.

They have lost sight of the 'more' of God and have stopped expecting, stopped encountering, and therefore are perpetuating religion.

Taking Back the Night

I love reading about the Israelites. They were a walking miracle of God. Once freed from captivity they were given manna daily. This was provision from Heaven that arrived every day. And the Bible says that they were only given as much as one day would allow. God wanted to meet their needs daily. He was big enough to meet all their needs every day. And water was given them. When there wasn't a spring or a source of water, then water would come from a rock – a miracle.

Yet they tired of the miracles. It was not enough. The Bible says that they began to grumble and complain; they had it better back in slavery. I cannot believe these people. Right before their eyes miracles are being performed. They are in the midst of what many today would call a revival. God is moving in their midst daily. The cloud of the glory of God was there, resting among them. Why then did it not satisfy?

Because it wasn't the fulfillment of the promise of God. The manna was good, and it was from God, but it wasn't a land flowing with milk and honey. It wasn't the promise. I see Christians every day who have tired of the manna of God. It is good; they are seeing miracles, they are seeing salvations, but it isn't the fulfillment of the promise.

How can someone experience such great miracles in their life and then, less than two years later, fall away? When they have settled for manna.

My dad always told me when I was growing up: good is a danger to best. We can so often settle for good, when God has a destiny of best for us. When we stop at good, we stop short of the fullness. Jesus could have prayed for the man with blindness and stopped when he said, "I see men walking around like trees." Jesus knew the promise, and he did not stop short of seeing it come about. Good will never take the place of best –

Supernatural Expectancy

God's best plan and destiny for us, me, this generation.

Many in the church have settled for less than the promises of God, and now there is a generation that is rising up saying we want more. Just like Joshua, they are beginning to look at the Promised Land and say, that is mine and I want it. It stirs the heart of God. He is looking for a generation that longs for the promises of God to be fulfilled and is willing to do something about it.

Joshua went to war. Will we?

He raised his expectancy level, and this came from an encounter with the Lord of Hosts. But he was driven to an encounter by desire, fueled by passion, which resulted in supernatural expectation. The wall will come down; the land will be ours.

When we operate out of function we only produce religion.

I remember one day receiving a call from a church outreach communications department. They said they had a new idea for church growth and wanted to know if I was interested in it. They called the new idea, "Simply ask." I said, "Why would I want this new idea?" "To grow your church, you should simply ask people to come," they said. "I am not interested," I said. They asked, "Why?" I said, "Because at our church we are part of the 'Simply Go' program. It was created by Christ, and He is still waiting for it to happen."

So many are inviting people to churches out of function. "Come to my church this Sunday." Why? "I don't know; it is something we are doing called Simply Ask."

WHEN WE OPERATE OUT OF FUNCTION WE ONLY PRODUCE RELIGION

Taking Back the Night

We have banners, promotional videos, flyers, pamphlets. I am sure that there are some who are going to get God in that program.

God uses a donkey when He has to, but there are good plans, and there are perfect plans. I want to be a part of the perfect plan of God, His perfect will. Simply Ask was for me another program, not a supernatural revelation.

I don't want to be a part of that. I don't tell people about my God because it is the latest thing we are doing at my church. I tell people about my God because you cannot keep me from telling people. I have a great God, a supernatural God who wants to impact your life and change your world. I am not doing this out of function; I am doing it because I have encountered the King of Kings and He has transformed my life.

An encounter births expectation. An encounter motivated by passion and birthed by longing.

Instead of trying to find another way of motivating people to finally tell others about God, maybe we should just get the church to encounter God and rediscover our original identity as the Bride of Christ – a warring Bride!

A young girl in our group got saved one night. She was a fallen away Catholic who encountered Jesus. He changed her life. I remember the night when she received the baptism of the Holy Spirit, just standing and worshipping. There were no hands laid on her; she just got God.

One Sunday Morning, I was standing in front of our church and she comes up and says she has fifteen people coming to church with her. Wow! I asked her why. She said, how could she not? After experiencing God so much and having Him transform her life, she just couldn't keep it to herself; it just

Supernatural Expectancy

wasn't right. That is an encounter – a supernatural encounter!

I don't function in healing – I expect healing!
I don't function in giving – I expect an open heaven!
I don't function in living – I live life more abundantly!

Let us no longer think this is it, but let us be stirred. Our God is the God of MORE! The God of abundance! The God of greatness! And we have been adopted into that kingdom.

I no longer walk as a pauper; I live as royalty who has access to the throne room!

Getting Focus

So often we lose the focus. We stop encountering because we take our eyes off of Christ, our hope of glory.

Where we look is vital in our expectancy level. Peter walked on water while he kept his eyes on Christ. The moment he looked away, he began to sink. When we stay focused on Christ we can operate and move in greater depths of the Spirit and power.

Where are you looking?

Inward looking is a breeding ground for a host of demonic viruses:
- Selfishness
- Bitterness
- Envy

The rich young ruler is a perfect example of inward looking. His question was a clear reflection of his heart. Yet Christ's answer held the power for a complete transformation. But where was he looking? Inward. His inward looking kept him from experiencing the very thing he was longing for.

So often I see Christians who are longing for an encounter

Taking Back the Night

with the Spirit, for God to come down, yet their focus keeps them from ever obtaining it. They look at their circumstances, their issues, what they have been through and they never truly realize who Christ is, because they are not looking at Him.

If the rich young ruler truly knew who was before him, then he would have sold all. Even if the young ruler's motivations were selfish, he would have realized here is the one who holds the keys to the storehouse. Here is the one who can provide all my needs. But his focus was off; he was a product of inner looking.

Backwards looking is a breeding ground for demonic strongholds:
- Regret
- Failure
- The should of's, could of's, would of's

When Jesus was faced with the man who wanted to go back and bury his father, His response was one that many would have felt was harsh, unfeeling and unsympathetic. "But Jesus said to him, 'Follow Me, and let the dead bury their own dead'" (Matthew 8:22).

I have heard many pastors preach on this section of Scripture, with amens from the congregation. Still, if we responded today as Jesus did, then our churches might be empty.

We cannot talk to people that way. We must comfort and coddle. If one from our congregation says they need to bury someone, we grab a shovel and go and help. Yet Jesus' response was, "Let the dead bury their own dead." Why?

It was an issue of focus. Where are we looking? That was backwards looking; the issues of the past. It was a representation of the old life, old bondages, old ways of thinking.

Christ was saying, you need a revelation in your looking.

Supernatural Expectancy

We are looking forward. We are no longer getting caught up in the issues of this life. I love what Leonard Ravenhill said, "This life is a dressing room for eternity." It is a glimpse, a moment, it is going to fade. We so often allow ourselves to get caught up in the issues of this life, when this life is fading and we need to be consumed with looking at Christ. What is He saying and what is He doing?

Left to right looking is a breeding ground for unhealthy motivations:
- Look at them
- Look at my circumstances

It can keep us from experiencing the fullness of what Christ has for us. When we look left to right, we may see what God is doing right now, but we get caught up in the moment and lose sight of the destiny.

Joseph is a perfect example. When his brothers came to him and begged for mercy, at that moment, inward looking could have kept him from fulfilling his destiny.

He could have allowed backwards looking to keep him from ever breaking free. He would have been in a vicious cycle of regret and second-guessing. I have heard over and over again that Joseph's pride got the better of him. He should have kept a servant mentality towards his brothers despite his dreams. That kind of thinking just continues to put more Christians in bondage. I don't live in the 'I should of,' I live in the, 'What now?' Whether Joseph should have kept his mouth shut or not, he never looked back and questioned it; he continued to move forward, because he knew what his destiny was.

The most dangerous of these three, for most Christians, is the left to right looking. When I see Joseph, he was in the midst of prison having revival. He could have stopped. This was God coming down. Dreams were being interpreted. Visions were coming. The glory was falling. There was favor. God was on the move. It was what we would class as a genuine move of God.

Often I have seen Christians stop at this point. God is moving all around them, and they have started looking left and right. They see the miracles, they see the movements, and they forget their destiny. They still don't realize that, like Joseph, they are in prison.

Joseph didn't stop because he knew that he was called to greater things. And we are called to greater things. We are the chosen generation. We are a royal priesthood. We have been called to proclaim the praise of God! We are not simply called to interpret some dreams – we are called to change the world around us.

Left to right looking lulls us into a false sense of fulfillment while destiny is passing us by. We cannot allow ourselves to settle for less than the fulfillment of His promise. I want the former and the latter rain to fall at once. I don't just want to see miracles in a church service, but also in the streets and in the schools. I don't want to get so caught up in what God does on Sunday morning that I stop looking for what God is longing to do on Monday morning.

Upward looking produces life. Before Jesus broke the bread to feed the five thousand, the Word says that He looked up. Why? Because He only does what He sees His Father is doing.

When we are involved in upward looking, we keep our eyes on the Father and we don't have to worry about seasons or streams, failure or success. We operate in a place that is in rhythm with the Father – supernatural rhythm.

Supernatural Expectancy

Why was Jesus' success rate flawless? He was still just a man. Yes, the Son of God, and still a man. So why was He so successful in healings, in the prophetic, in all that He did? He lived in a constant state of communion with the Father. He never let His eyes falter. He was a product of only upward looking, upward focus.

I have been accused by some in today's culture of being narrowly focused. Even some Christians have said that {Gasp}. Yet Christ was completely focused. He was focused directly on God. And God holds all eternity in His hands. I don't call that narrow; I call that wisdom. I call that intimacy.

I will never have eyes for another woman. Is that narrow focused? That is marriage. God is looking for the church to be that Bride, to be so focused on Him, so infatuated and in love with who He is.

In that moment, we will not have to wait for seasons of harvest, of outpouring or healings. We will have springs in the wilderness, we will see rain during drought, and we will reap a double portion of the harvest because we are in rhythm with the Spirit.

Why does this matter so much? When I look at the story of the ten lepers, I see an amazing revelation. In Luke 17, we have ten lepers who cry out to Christ to be healed. He tells them to go and present themselves before the priests, and as they went they were healed.

That is awesome. But there was more that Jesus wanted to do than just heal them. You see, all of them had an encounter with Christ, but only one of them was Christ-focused. In verse 17, seeing that only one returns to give Him thanks, He has an amazing response:

> Jesus asked, "Were not all ten cleansed? Where are

the other nine? Was no one found to return and give praise to God except this foreigner?" Then he said to him, "Rise and go; **your faith has made you well.**" (Luke 17:17-19, emphasis added, NIV)

We see this over and over again with Jesus. He does not simply want to heal the body, but to make us whole. This wholeness in spirit requires a focus on Christ.

Real Encounters

So how could someone have an encounter and walk away from it all? If we count the costs, and decide that we cannot afford the risk.

When an encounter is only skin deep, we find that we can peel back that layer of skin and operate in pain for a season. I don't want that. I would rather die in this life and have a lifetime of eternal, blissful living with the Father.

The world is waiting for encounters that will sear them.

There is a generation waiting in the darkness that has found they have nothing left. They have nothing else to live for, and they are willing to give all that they have for the cause. These are not unknowns to God. He has led nations with them.

Like Moses they have wandered the wilderness looking for truth, looking for a burning bush. We are called to be that burning bush to a lost and dying generation. We are the light and power that they are longing to encounter.

I remember the night that Shelby walked into Club Retro. So many come into the Club, so often, that it is hard to keep track of them all. Different nights of the week, hundreds of young people, changing from day to day. But when she came in, I knew that God was going to hit her. What it would look

Supernatural Expectancy

like and how it would happen did not bother me. I simply shone, because I am a light.

I remember stamping her hand as she walked into the building, and moving on. There was a line of young people behind her waiting to get in. She passed by, nothing appeared to have happened.

It wasn't till later that night that she grabbed me and told me her life had to change. I knew this much, but I still didn't understand it fully.

I found out later that Shelby came from a Christian background, but one rooted in religion. She had gone to church; she just had not encountered God. Her life was spinning out of control. That day, she had decided she was going to end her life. It was no longer worth living for. She had just enough God to make living in the world miserable, so she was just going to stop living.

Her family knew that something needed to change, she needed something that they were not offering. Out of desperation they encouraged her to come to Club Retro. Normally she would have said no. This was not somewhere she would ever have hung out, these were not "her people." But tonight it did not matter anymore, one last hoorah before she ended it all.

What she didn't know was that Club Retro was at a church, and that God was setting her up in a direct path for an encounter – a supernatural encounter.

This was more than just Christians loving her into Heaven. I remember when she looked me in the eyes. I thought, "This girl is crazy." Then, "She is going to fit right in." She had grabbed me by the shoulders and said, you have no idea what has happened to me tonight. I didn't. But I would soon find out.

She told me that she had written a suicide note. That it was all planned, and she was ready to end her life. God had other plans.

Taking Back the Night

When she walked through the door and I stamped her hand, she felt the supernatural power of God and it literally transformed her.

Light transforms the darkness around it. This book shouldn't really be called *Taking Back the Night*. Because you never take back night; you transform it. Light brings about transformation in darkness, or so it should.

I have had people walk into Club Retro and get thrown backwards as they enter the building, because of the presence of God.

I was stamping one girl's hand as she came in, and when I stamped her, she pulled her hand back in shock. I asked her what the problem was, and she said that she felt a fire go through her hand and arm. The presence of God is real, tangible and powerful, and we have it, and the world needs to experience it.

PART 4
Transforming the Night

The darkness does not comprehend the light,

but in its embrace, it is transformed.

- 14 -

A LOVE ENCOUNTER

I have met many people who say that Christians should love people into Heaven. Where did we get this concept? Now, before you spill your argument into a book, I know God is love and that the greatest commandment is love. We are supposed to love our neighbors. I know that 1 John says that those that do not love do not know God for God is love.

We could be here for a long time simply talking about love. Yet I do not believe that love is the encounter we are supposed to be giving a dying world. I believe that the world is in need of a powerful supernatural encounter. The physical manifestation of the power of God, motivated by love.

So often we have given the world an encounter of love, motivated by love. What does that look like? I like to chalk that up to simply good deeds. We love our community or our neighbors by being friendly, painting a wall, helping them move, watching their kids, getting involved in the local clubs, sports groups, schools, community events.

We must 'show the love of God' to those around us. Yet I think we have failed to grasp what a true love encounter with God is supposed to look like. Don't get me wrong, good deeds are great. Yet good deeds can be accomplished by any sinner. My problem with the goal of loving people by being good, or nice, is that as Christians we are in trouble. We have boxed ourselves into acts of function again, which produces religion.

I know many unsaved people who are nicer and sweeter than me. Just being good or involved in your community can be achieved by anyone. Many churches have become nothing more effective than the Girl Scouts, or the local Rotary Club. We are nice people doing nice things for the community, yet we say it is the love of God.

In the city where I grew up, the Mormon church was much more effective in being involved in the community than any of the Christian churches. If we mark it up to how many walls we paint, then we are in trouble.

Goodness does not always equate to Godness. I used to joke that I was going to make a bumper sticker that said, "Good people go to hell." Because it is true; I know a lot of good people who still need a God encounter.

> GOODNESS DOES NOT ALWAYS EQUATE TO GODNESS

So what is love supposed to look like? Well, I always like to go back to the simple things, the most popular verse in America. John 3:16, "For God so loved the world that He gave His only Son that whosoever should believe in Him shall not perish but have everlasting life."

God so loved the world that He operated in power! Love is always meant to be the motivation, and power was always meant to be the expectation. Yes, love is the end result, but anyone can paint a wall; the power of Christ changes lives.

Does that mean we don't paint walls? I always used to say,

A Love Encounter

God I don't want to just paint walls. Then one day He woke me up and said, you are going to paint a wall, just paint it in power. Transform the atmosphere around you. Bind the strong man, cast out demons, heal the sick. Freely you have received so freely give.

All throughout the Gospels, you see Jesus, motivated by love, giving those around Him a power encounter. He sees a man with leprosy, and motivated by love, He heals him. He sees blind eyes, the lame, the broken, the hurting. Out of compassion, out of love, He moves in power.

Even when it comes to feeding those without food, it took a complete act of power to see it happen. Christ was not fooled. He knew that a dying world needed an encounter with power. They don't simply need another Gandhi. Anyone can attempt to be good through their actions, but it takes an act of God to transform a region. It takes an act of power.

That is why we have the fruits of the Spirit *and* the gifts of the Spirit. Combined, they make a powerful combination, one that sends fear into the enemy. Yet, mixing the fruits of the Spirit, as motivation, with the fruits of the Spirit, as expectation, creates frustration and ultimately agitation.

Mixing the gifts as motivation with gifts as expectation creates sensationalism. I have seen this as well. The sensationalist Christians can literally make the heart of God sick. They are those who stand before the throne saying, "Look what I did." And God responds back, "I never knew you." When we get into sensationalism, the feel-good wows, we can often miss the character of God – His love, His fruits.

What we need is proper motivation – love, compassion, the heart of Christ for a dying world. Jesus said, no greater love is there but to give your life for a friend. Jesus' ultimate act of love was an ultimate act of power.

The world does not need another encounter with simply good people. They need an encounter with powerful people. That is what God created us to be – a powerful people. We have the same power that raised Jesus from the grave living inside of us. For what purpose? To love people? No, to encounter people. It is love that has put that power in us, and love that should be the reason we use it.

This is a dangerous concept. I have seen Christians who operate in power without love, and the end result is not pretty. Sure, there may be some fruit; God uses willing vessels. Yet there is something about the ministry or person that reeks of personal agenda, false motivations. The power of the encounter is diminished by the flesh.

This is the difficulty with the fruits and the gifts. It is so easy to operate in one or the other without much death to self. The combination of the two requires true intimacy with Christ; less of me, and more of Him. Death to sin, self, and flesh – more often than not, a painful process.

- 15 -

THE POWER OF PRESENCE

How do we obtain this amazing power that we are supposed to operate in? Love is somewhat easy. Almost anyone can paint a wall. But how do we get this power?

Presence = Power

Whenever you see examples of the presence of God, you see the power of God. The Holy Spirit is represented many times in the Bible as a person of power: fire, wind and water.

One of the things that transformed me early on in my walk was when I read about the amazing encounter that Moses had with God. In Exodus 33, Moses climbs up the mountain and meets with God. God tells Moses that He is angry with the people so He is sending an angel to go with them on the next leg of their journey.

That sounds cool – an angel! This is God speaking. He is telling Moses this is the way it is. I am sending an angel, because if I came down I would consume my people.

Yet, Moses is not moved by God's decision. In fact, he stands in direct opposition to what God just said. He stands before the Lord of Hosts and says, if your presence does not go with us do not take us from this place (Exodus 33:15). Why does he say that? The answer is in verse 16: "For how then will it be known that Your people and I have found grace in Your sight, except You go with us? So we shall be separate, Your people and I, from all the people who are upon the face of the earth" (Exodus 33:16, NKJV).

Moses knew what he was doing. He knew what the real heart of God was. The people of God should always be marked by the presence of God, and presence equals power! Throughout the journey through the wilderness, the people of God were always marked by the supernatural power of God. It says that a cloud went before them by day and a fire by night.

This is what separated them from all the others on the earth. The physical manifest presence of God. And we should still be experiencing that today. Somewhere along the way, God said I am sending an angel, and we accepted it and settled for less than the presence of God. Yet, there are those who are rising and saying, no more! They are standing at the gates of the throne room and demanding the presence of God. That language, that tone can be offensive to those who have grown up in a sheltered Christian lifestyle.

> IF WE SAY THAT WE ARE A PEOPLE OF GOD THEN OTHERS SHOULD BE ABLE TO LOOK FROM THE OUTSIDE AND SEE GOD IS AMONG US

They stand back aghast, shocked that anyone would talk to God in that way. Yet, it is those very cries, that very passion and desire that moves the heart of God.

If we are going to say that we are a people of God, then others should be able to look from the outside and see that God is among us.

The Power Of Presence

If we long to bring the light into the darkness, then we are going to have to pursue and possess the presence of God. When Moses encountered God, it affected everything around him. Nothing could stay the same. It didn't mean everything was easy. Quite the opposite; it meant there was a war going on.

- 16 -

THE REVIVAL FORMULA

I have been accused of manipulating the Spirit, stirring things up that are not even there. I thought, wow, what a great accusation!

If we could somehow manipulate the presence of God to come down, who would not do it every day all day long? The reality is that the only formula I know is passion, desire, and repentance. Throw those things together in any order and you will grab the attention of the throne room.

Sure, I just summed up what many authors have written whole books about, and there may be more to come. Yet, with my own eyes, I have seen the glory come down with any mixture of those three ingredients. They may be ugly, unpolished and raw, yet the glory is the same, and in the end it is beautiful.

For a few years, I was privileged to sit at the table of the revival in Brownsville, Florida. During its height, I saw the lines of the desperate standing for hours to get in and experience the mighty move of God. It gave me a perspective on what revival really means.

In 2008, an outpouring began to fall in Lakeland, Florida. Here is an email I sent out to a revival mailing list of a few

Taking Back the Night

thousand people in response to the Lakeland Revival:

> Allow me to stir a bit of hunger.
>
> The last few weeks at Family, in Orangevale, Sacramento....we have seen some amazing things transpire. I have been there when ears have opened. I have felt tumors dissolve. We have seen a trend of cancer patients completely set free.
>
> I have been thrown off my feet by the power of God. I have wept openly in stores and restaurants as the glory filled the room. I have been unable to move, and so frustrated that I couldn't be stopped. I have been truly broken and am completely desperate.
>
> We are ruined - Yet...
>
> If the choice was, come to Sacramento and become satisfied, I would rather you stay home and become desperate. I want what is in Lakeland, Toronto, Bethel, Africa, South America, Heaven. But I want to hunger.
>
> Blessed are those who hunger.........for they shall be filled.
>
> I am excited, but I am not even tempted yet. You cannot appease me with the samplings of the very thing we are called to do. I am not in awe of talents, but am floored by the glory. I do not seek merely a moment but a transformation. Not of just me, but of the world around me.
>
> This outpouring is not to be contained in

The Revival Formula

the four walls of church or religion.

It was not meant to be simply sampled and regurgitated in churches around America.

I would pray that it would stir hunger that THERE IS MORE!

I don't see what others do and say "let me duplicate!"

I see what others do and am filled with supernatural jealousy that I have been missing out on the MORE! And I WANT IT!

GO! Go wherever you need to go to be stirred. To allow hunger, passion, desperation to rise, but please do not settle. To not feel as though - Yes, I have done that now!

What have we done! Gone somewhere?

We have a world longing for a transformation, crying out for a visitation. And we have a God longing for His glory to fill the whole earth!

When we settle - we fail! No - I will not stop in the pursuit of the fullness of the promise of God!

I have seen amazing things and have yet to see anything!

I have experienced the power of the glory of the Lord and yet I have experienced nothing!

I am full - yet I am starving!

GOD - I want more!

What is taking place in Sacramento has amazed

me – and yes has begun to really transform all that is around us – so what now... well done? Pat on the back? Good job? NO! I want more!

We are just barely scratching the surface – and this is not a scratch and sniff sticker movement – our God is bigger than that and there is more to be had. So please, radicals – those still reading and not totally offended!

Let us cry out for more – because it is that very hunger that has moved the heart of God to pour at this moment, and it is that hunger, that desperation, that desire that is going to cause God to rend the heavens and allow something even greater. Like the fullness of the promises of God to come forth – The former rain and the latter rain!

The very fact that we can experience can create luke-warmness. Oh that we would be seared.

Desperate and hungry

Matthew Oliver - In pursuit of the chef – tired of sitting at the table

In Mark 7:24-30, we see a woman who finds out that Jesus is visiting her community. This woman is desperate; she needs her daughter to be healed. When she finds out where Jesus is, she comes and falls at His feet, begging Him to heal her daughter, to cast out the demon.

The words that are used here are amazing. She begged Him

The Revival Formula

to set her daughter free. She petitioned the Lord to move. She laid her demand on the table and begged for God to hear her cry.

Jesus' response is shocking. Look at verse 27: "Let the children be filled first, for it is not good to take the children's bread and throw it to the little dogs."

He says no! Jesus Christ tells the woman no. He doesn't even do it nicely. He calls her a dog. Why? This goes all the way back to how your encounter with God will define you. Can Jesus do it? Yes. Will it cost Him anything to do it? No. He is God. The healing is not the issue; the deliverance is not the issue. The outpouring is not the issue – God is longing to know about the heart.

I have come before the throne of God and begun to cry out for the promised outpouring, that the glory of the Lord would cover the whole earth. And just like the Syro-Phoenician woman, I will not stop until I get the fullness of the promise.

When Jesus told her no, she persisted. Even the dogs eat the scraps from the children's table! I think Jesus was blessed. She really wanted it. He saw the desire and desperation in her heart; she was broken and longing, and she would not leave with anything less than freedom.

We want revival, but so often we want it on our terms, on our timetables. God come down, but do it in this three-hour service. I think there are days that God is just fed up with listening to the restraints of man. He wants to know, "How badly do My people want it?" He is looking for hunger, He is looking for desperation. He is looking for desire that moves the heart of God.

The Syro-Phoenician woman did not change the mind of Christ; she just tapped into His heart.

Taking Back the Night

When Moses was on the mountain in Exodus 32, God had become angry with the Israelites. So he tells Moses, in verse 10, "Now leave me alone so that my anger may burn against them and that I may destroy them. Then I will make you into a great nation" (NIV). Here you have God telling Moses what He is going to do. And Moses doesn't stand for it. He begins to intercede on behalf of this nation. Why? Because he knew the heart of God. He begins to petition the throne: Your name is at stake; this is Your people. And God hears His cry.

That is what we do now. We petition on behalf of God's heart: we are Your people; Your name is at stake; this is Your promise. We hold God accountable to the very word that He has spoken.

James 4:2 says that you do not have because you do not ask. We know that God will give us the desires of our heart; Psalms 37:4 says that. That does not mean we get everything we want. If you finish reading James 4:3, it says, "You ask and do not receive, because you ask amiss, that you may spend it on your pleasures."

When do we get the desires of our heart? When they are God's desires. There is a place of such intimacy with God that you can feel His heartbeat. We can get in such rhythm with the very heart of God, with what moves and motivates Him. What brings Him joy and what grieves Him. When we find that rhythm, we hear that heartbeat and we begin to pray the very heart of God back to Him. It moves Him to action.

Do you want revival? So does God. He just wants to know how badly you want it. Because His heart is not to send something that is momentary or that stays in a church building. His heart is to transform the world – "let the whole earth be filled with His glory" (Psalm 72:19). He doesn't want His glory to have to

The Revival Formula

fit into worldly concepts and schemes. He wants to transform the world into His glory. So He waits. The promise still remains and it is still as vibrant today as the day it was spoken. He is testing the heart.

- 17 -

HEAVEN ON EARTH

I have petitioned the throne and asked God to come down; God let Your glory fall.

Let's look at a few of the promises. What is it that we are longing for? So often, as Christians, we settle for much less than the fullness of what God has intended for us. We end at eternal life, when there is so much more to be tasted in the kingdom of God.

I mentioned in the opening of the book about the young man with the Mohawk, who started me on a part of this wild adventure. He said, what good is eternal life to me now, I am not dead? That opened the door for an amazing revelation about eternal life.

Eternal life is the door prize to Christianity. Everybody gets it, and it is just the beginning. It was never meant to be the sum of our Christian walk. We are now saved and going to Heaven, so we think we have nothing else on this earth.

I am always amazed by Christians who are constantly longing to go to Heaven. When I read the Bible, I see a God who is constantly trying to get out of Heaven. He is longing to be with His people. He wants relationship. We can have that now.

Taking Back the Night

I am not entertained with the idea of being taken to a third heaven. I want what Jesus said, let "Your kingdom come". Let "Your will be done on Earth as it is in Heaven" (Matthew 6:10). I do not need to be taken up; I want God to come down.

That is a promise that we have. Eternal life is good, but we have so much more that we can experience now; we simply have to ask. It is the Father's heart to give good gifts.

Joel 2:23 says that He will give us the "former rain and the latter rain" in the same month. Matthew 10:8 says we are to raise the dead, cleanse the leper, cast out demons. Joshua 1:3 tells us that everywhere we go God has already given us.

We could write many books on the promises of God. Promises of healing (1 Peter 2:24; Psalm 103:3), and protection (Psalm 23:4; Hebrews 13:6). Promises of comfort (John 14:27; Isaiah 26:3), and guidance (Proverbs 3:5, Psalm 37:23). Support (Psalm 9:10; 2 Cor. 4:9) and encouragement (Romans 8:35). Promises that we will not be given more than we can bear (1 Cor. 10:13).

These are promises for us as Christians, yet there are also promises for the land and for the transforming of the world around us.

One of the most prominent promises I hear thrown around is from Joel:

"And afterward,

I will pour out my Spirit on all people.
Your sons and daughters will prophesy,
your old men will dream dreams,
your young men will see visions.

Even on my servants, both men and women,
I will pour out my Spirit in those days.

Heaven On Earth

I will show wonders in the heavens
and on the earth…" (Joel 2:28-30, NIV)

Here is a promise of God. Yet, I am often baffled when I talk to Christians who want to experience this, but just don't want to do anything to receive it. The promises of God are not like the love of God. The love of God is unconditional; the promises of God are not.

Let me use provision as an example. God says that He will provide for us according to His riches and glory. Yet, we have all seen Christians struggling with finances. So is God a liar? No, the Bible says that His promises are yes and amen (so be it). What we have to do is pair it with the action scripture that says give and it shall be given back to you (Luke 6:38). So there are keys to unlocking the promises of God.

> WHEN I READ THE BIBLE, I SEE A GOD WHO IS CONSTANTLY TRYING TO GET OUT OF HEAVEN

The love of God is unconditional. He says that He will never leave us nor forsake us, that nothing can separate us from the love of God. Yet, His promises ask for action on our part. When I look at that scripture in Joel, I get excited, but the scripture starts off, in verse 28 with, *afterward*. If God is saying *afterward* then that means there must be a before. That means we do something and *then* He pours out His Spirit.

There is action that is required. If we look a little earlier in the same chapter;

"Even now," declares the LORD,
"return to me with all your heart,

Taking Back the Night

with fasting and weeping and mourning."

Rend your heart
and not your garments.
Return to the LORD your God,
for he is gracious and compassionate,
slow to anger and abounding in love,
and he relents from sending calamity. (Joel 2:12-13, NIV)

This is the action God was asking of the people. Begin to cry out. Do you long for the promise of revival and the fulfillment of the Scriptures? Do you long to invade the darkness like a warrior, and rise up and see the light of glory shine into this land? Then begin to pursue the heart of God, and go out and see it happen. Put it into action.

- 18 -

THE POWER OF WAITING

It is vital that we understand the concept of waiting. As a pastor, I am frustrated with the Christians who sit back and say that they are waiting on God. I always get this scripture brought up:

> But those who **wait on the LORD**
> Shall renew their strength;
> They shall mount up with wings like eagles,
> They shall run and not be weary,
> They shall walk and not faint. (Isaiah 40:31, emphasis added)

I am waiting on God to move. That is what I am told all the time. I don't want to move without God moving. And then, as a pastor I have to come back with, it is always easier to steer a moving ship.

Then God showed me something about waiting. The word for waiting used by Isaiah was the Hebrew word *Qavah* - eagerly expecting; to anticipate; to look for.

Well that throws a wrench into the American idea of waiting. We see waiting as sitting on our butt until God does something. God sees waiting as us passionately pursuing His presence. That scripture sounds very different if we read it as, "They that passionately pursue the presence of the Lord shall renew their strength. They shall mount up with wings like eagles, they shall run and not be weary, they shall walk and not faint."

There is a generation rising that is no longer settling for our comfortable concepts of Christianity and God. And we have a God that is moving and no longer operating in the religious box that we have tried to place Him in. I am not saying that God will move without the church; I simply believe that the church does not look like what we think it looks like. There is a shift taking place.

This has nothing to do with cell churches, home churches, mega churches, seeker churches. This has to do with the Bride of Christ, and God is awakening His Bride. The earth is groaning, there is a travailing from the dark that is crying out for the glory of the Lord, and it must be answered.

That groaning is being met by the cry of a new generation. A generation that is not marked by income, color or status, but one that is noted for its unwavering willingness to give up all in its pursuit of the heart of God. That generation has moved the King to action. That generation has put a demand on the throne, and called down the rain. That generation has tipped the scales, and the water is beginning to pour. The light is beginning to invade the darkness.

PART 5
A New Breed of Warriors

*To become victorious,
one must first engage in a battle.*

- 19 -
A CHOSEN GENERATION

"But you are a **chosen generation**, a royal priesthood, a holy nation, His own special people, that you may proclaim the praises of Him who called you out of darkness into His marvelous light" (1 Peter 2:9, emphasis added).

That scripture was written nearly two thousand years ago. I am often asked the question, which generation is the chosen one? We cannot all be chosen, isn't there one generation that will be *the* generation to usher in the presence of God, so that His glory fills the whole earth?

I have a few thoughts on this. Firstly, I do believe that many generations can be the chosen generation. We can all be chosen, we can all be adopted into the royalty of God, and we are all called to proclaim the praise of God. Has every generation done that? That is for Heaven to answer, but there is a difference between being *chosen* and being *called*.

> A CHOSEN GENERATION IS ONE THAT LAYS HOLD OF THE PROMISES OF GOD

Many are called, but few are chosen (Matthew 22:14). I

believe that a *chosen* generation is the generation that lays hold of the promises of God and does not relent until they see them in their fullness.

When I read 1 Corinthians, I find out what it means to be *chosen*: "God chose the foolish things of the world to shame the wise; God chose the weak things of the world to shame the strong. He chose the lowly things of this world and the despised things – and the things that are not – to nullify the things that are" (1 Cor. 1:27-28, NIV).

When I look at Revelation 17:14, I see that there are those who are called, those who are chosen, and those who are faithful:

> "These will make war with the Lamb, and the Lamb will overcome them, for He is Lord of lords and King of kings; and those who are with Him are called, chosen, and faithful." (Revelations 17:14)

Everyone is called, but being chosen is our response. The *chosen* generation is the one that hears the call of the Lord. It is the same call that Isaiah heard, "Who will go and whom will I send?" It is that echoing call of Heaven for a generation to rise up and take hold of its destiny and begin to transform the earth with the glory of God. You are the light, shine!

- 20 -

THE LIVING DEAD

Dead men have no wants. Dead men have no desires. Dead men have no needs.

These are some of the statements that we scrawled across a t-shirt that was designed for *Consecrated*, our worship band. On the front of one of our shirts was the word "DIE!" Bold and in your face. In small print it said, "Living to die, dying to live."

That is our motto, what we live by. I do not believe we have truly understood the reality of dying to oneself. We have tried to make formulas for dying. Growing up, I saw a vampire movie called *Lost Boys*. In it one of the characters said that no two vampires ever die the same way. They all die differently, and you never know what to expect.

Well, I'm not getting my inspiration from a vampire movie, but there is no real formula for dying, yet you normally know when you are dead.

The apostle Paul said, "I affirm, by the boasting in you which I have in Christ Jesus our Lord, I die daily" (1 Cor. 15:31). Jesus told His disciples to take up their cross and follow Him, twice (Matthew 10:38 and 16:24). Then He goes on to say, whoever loses His life for My sake will find it.

Taking Back the Night

Learning to lose one's life is actually a pursuit that holds power. It was such a great conquest that Paul attempted it daily. I have already said that there is a generation that is longing to live for something worth dying for. The question is: are we willing to die while living?

I posed a question to our group one night. If Jesus said that we would do greater things than Him, what is greater than giving one's life in death? My answer was – giving one's life while still living.

There is a cry that is rising for the *living dead*. There is a generation that is no longer consumed with self and self-indulgence. This goes against the grain of popular culture, and it even bucks the concepts that most churches operate in.

I have decided that the American dream is not necessarily God's desire for me as a Christian. We have these preconceived notions as Christians in America that things should be a certain way or that we should be able to live a certain way and have certain things. Yet, that is not always God's perfect plan for us. Does God long for us to prosper? Sure, I will take all that He will give me. But more than that, He longs to encounter us and for us to have the character to sustain our destiny in Him.

We have gone for the goods without the God. As I tell Christians all the time, happiness is not guaranteed in the Bible. I think God longs for us to be happy, but that is only a by-product of finding the heart of God. When we truly learn to die, we will learn to find the heart of God and experience true happiness. We will find that it is not stuff, or circumstances, but a state of supernatural faith.

One of the greatest attacks in current secular culture and in the church in America is that everyone wants to be served, but no one wants to do the serving. Oh, we don't mind serving

The Living Dead

when it fits our agenda, yet the whole purpose of serving is to operate in a kingdom mentality that declares war on the enemy.

A teaching that corrupted church life in America for a while was the concept of the round table. That we are all equals. The idea of the round table, in the story of King Arthur, was that all the knights were equal and all had equal input into every decision and every battle.

Yet, my Bible talks about a kingdom mentality. One that says we are a body and that all parts are important, but if the hand started telling the heart how to pump blood, we would all be dead. Or if my foot decided to tell my mouth how to eat, I would starve. In a kingdom you have a king who speaks to the rest of the kingdom. A king who sets the goals, lays the plans and orders the ways of the kingdom.

We are an army, in a kingdom where we have commanders, generals and lieutenants. There are prophets and apostles, teachers, pastors and evangelists. We need the Godly order if we want to operate with success.

God operates as the King of this kingdom, His kingdom. Not one of flesh and blood, not one that will fade away, a kingdom that is eternal. He has drawn the lines and set the boundaries for His kingdom to operate within. Boundaries like free will and choice. Boundaries like using His vessels for His will. In His kingdom He has a divine order that He operates in, that He moves within, that creates accountability, covering and authority.

When we begin to operate in this kingdom mentality, we release an increase in the supernatural. We are releasing kingdom authority, and in doing so, we establish His kingdom on this earth. One not made of flesh and blood and one that cannot easily be broken down.

Taking Back the Night

There are many Christians who don't want to be told what to do by anyone. They take the attitude that if God wants to talk to them, then He'd better come down from Heaven and speak to them directly.

I think God is fed up with that mentality and is bypassing the whole process. There is a generation out there that is willing to die daily. They are no longer concerned with their own personal agenda. Their personal desires, longings and wants have been replaced by the heart of God.

Remember that for God to increase, we must decrease.

Death to self is not easy; if it was it wouldn't be called death. Yet, it is in that place of complete abandon that we find the supernatural presence of God shining forth. When you let His desire consume you, you are no longer concerned with living, and you press into the throne room to find that you are no longer that person you once were. You have been transformed, from glory to glory.

I remember a time of crushing I went through. It started in a cellphone store. I was standing there when a young woman came in with hearing aids in both of her ears. God told me right then and there to pray for her. I argued with God for a period of time. This wasn't church; this wasn't Sunday morning. What was He thinking?

> IN THAT PLACE OF COMPLETE ABANDON WE FIND THE SUPERNATURAL PRESENCE OF GOD SHINING FORTH

Regrettably, I won that argument and not only did I lose out, but the young lady left without receiving her encounter with God. God began to challenge me that day. I wanted the

The Living Dead

glory to fall; I just didn't want to have to do anything to bring it. Hunger and desire began to rise up inside of me. I was grieved that I had not prayed for the young woman. I was stricken at night with compassion and desire for God's destiny. The fact that I hadn't acted ruined me, and I asked God to give me another opportunity to pray for someone who was deaf. I began to have the desire to see ears open outside of the church.

Not long after that, I was standing in the return line at a home improvement store. There was an older couple in front of me, and the man had two hearing aids. I felt the unction of the Spirit to pray for him. So I asked the man's wife if I could pray for him, and after a moment of decision, she said yes. It was at that moment that God hijacked me. He spoke right into my heart, "Place your fingers in the man's ears."

"What?" What was God thinking? I had just gotten the courage to pray for him, and now He wanted me to stick my fingers in his ears.

"Stick your fingers in his ears, and get your fingers wet first."

"What? GOD!" He wanted me to lick my fingers and stick them in this man's ears, in the middle of the store, in the middle of the day?

God began to ask me, "How badly do you want it?" I knew that it had nothing to do with fingers in ears, or licking fingers. It had to do with death to my self, and how badly I wanted it. At that point, I wanted it really bad. It had consumed me; it had ruined me.

When you are truly dead, nothing else matters. Not fingers in ears, not licking fingers, nothing. Or so I thought.

I briefly told the couple that what I was about to do might seem a bit odd, but that I was just following orders from God.

Taking Back the Night

I quickly licked both fingers and placed them in his ears, and began praying a prayer that sounded something like this, "Oh God please, if I have never asked anything from you before, please heal this guy, so that I didn't just stick my spit-covered fingers in his ears for nothing."

After a few moments of praying with my fingers in his ears, I pulled out the fingers and looked at the man and I knew, just as he knew, that nothing had happened.

I went home that day completely crushed. I was angry at God. I didn't know if I was more angry that the guy did not get healed or that I was made to look like a fool. Then God had the gall to ask me if I would do it again. Never, I decided. If He wasn't going to heal, then I wasn't going to pray.

A day later, I was standing in another store, and a young woman came in, hearing aids in her ears. I felt the stirring in my heart. "Not this time," I told God. But the stirring persisted. I was so ruined. I was so not my own person; I was God's. If I was not living for me, then who was I living for? So I told God, if I pray for her, you have to heal her.

Again, I stuck two spit-covered fingers into this poor girl's ears, and prayed, and cried, and... nothing happened. You could ask the question why, and I would be there with you. I don't know, but I know that God is looking for obedience from His people. Simple obedience.

I used to say that God is looking for stupid people, because some of the things he has asked me to do, no person in their right mind would ever do. But that is not the case. He is looking for dead people. And if you are not dead yet, don't worry, the fire of God, that fire that burns in us and makes us shine, it can kill you. It burns away the flesh until all that is left is the glory.

That young lady did not get healed, and God and I argued

The Living Dead

again, and I made another proclamation that I would never pray for anyone like that again. Then I found myself in our local grocery store, just around the corner from our church. I know the manager; I know the clerks and the baggers. I had a cart full of groceries, and as I got in line to check out, there in front of me was a little girl signing to her mom.

She was deaf, and she needed my Jesus, and God was asking me, how about this time? I would love to say that I jumped at the chance, but I waited. God, I know this place, they know me. Then I stopped. They know You. They know that I represent You, and it is no longer my name on the line, it is Yours.

It shifted that quickly for me. I found I was dead. At that moment, I would have stuck my fingers in anyone's ears, but what I cared about was my God – His reputation, His glory. At that moment I asked the little girl's mom if I could pray for her. She said yes, and I didn't even bother explaining. I just stuck these two wet fingers in her ears, and I began to praise my God.

Not two seconds passed and the little girl began to scream. "I can hear, I can hear!" She began to shout. The whole aisle was filled with people as this little girl was shouting. I stood back, as they gathered round her, and I thanked my God. I was gone, and then God showed up.

That is the *living dead*. I have prayed for countless ears to be opened now, and seen amazing healings. I just learned to die.

There is a whole world out there waiting for the *living dead*, for lights to shine in the darkness.

- 21 -

BLOOD THIRSTY

Joshua was a different breed of warrior. He looked at the promise, and he was consumed by it. He didn't let his current circumstances dictate to him how he was going to react or respond. He encountered God and then fanatically pursued the promise, and would not stop short of it no matter what. He simply obeyed when God spoke, no matter how bizarre, no matter how extreme, and he understood the principles of a kingdom mentality.

Joshua was so confident in his God, and the faithfulness of the promise of God, that it shocked him when they lost the battle of Ai. I love Joshua's petition before the throne. He meets with God and in Joshua 7:9, he tells the Lord, *they will surround us and wipe out our name from the earth. What then will you do for your own great name?*

God, this is your promise, and we are your people, and it is your name at stake! What are you going to do? Joshua has so committed himself to the pursuit of God and His promises, that he has nothing left but the name of his God. What a great place to be!

There is a new breed of warriors that is rising. They have

seen the promises of our fathers fall to the wayside, and they are longing to restore glory to the house.

In Joshua 14 verse 6, we see Caleb coming to Joshua. He is eighty-five years old, but he is still clinging to a promise. He has spent his life serving Joshua and God. Fighting on behalf of another's vision, living a life serving others. Yet he had a promise; he was bloodthirsty.

In verse 8, Caleb reminds Joshua of the promise that God had given him through Moses, that everywhere his feet walked would be a part of his inheritance, and he wanted it. I love the way he speaks in verses 11 and 12: "I am still as strong today as the day Moses sent me out; I'm just as vigorous to go out to battle now as I was then. Now give me this hill country that the LORD promised me that day" (Joshua 14:11-12, NIV).

He puts a demand on God to fulfill the promise. He understood covenant, he understood promise, and he was a warrior.

When I look at this new army that is rising, I am reminded of 1 Kings 20. The king of Aram has gathered his army to attack King Ahab and the Israelites. Ahab is afraid and outnumbered, so he calls on the prophet. The prophet comes with the word of the Lord and tells the King to gather the *young men* from the provinces.

These were the young generation that had been scattered. They were outcasts. They were the unwanted ones. They had been sent out of the city to the extreme edges of the region. And now God was saying, I will defeat this enemy with the very things that you have scattered from your land. This is My chosen generation. This is a new breed of warrior.

This young army was extreme, passionate, and wild, and they were bloodthirsty. They led the army of the Israelites, and

Blood Thirsty

before the rest of the army had arrived, the young warriors had each killed their own opponent. They didn't wait for the army; they knew their destiny and the promise of their God and they took it, and with it they brought glory to the King.

God is in the process of calling the outcasts, and those who have been turned away by the functions of church. Those who look different and dress different. They have been bred in the darkness of night but redeemed by the light, and are longing to shine. Those the church does not understand. God is calling them in as a wild generation. They will go forth ahead of the church and begin to slay the enemy. They are hungry for a battle, they are desirous for a confrontation, and they rejoice in God's victory.

They are not waiting for that massing of the army of the Lord. They are sent out, not as rogue agents, but as a warring Bride, united in passion, desire and death. They no longer fight for themselves but for the call and the cause, and they have honed and crafted weapons of warfare long-forgotten by the church. They have unearthed the ancient ways of the supernatural and are wielding the flaming torch of truth that sears the darkness.

- 22 -

AN EXTREME GENERATION

The potential damage this new army that is rising can wreak upon the enemy is insurmountable. The darkness has yet to grasp the effect that light can have upon it. Still, the enemy has caught on quicker than the church to the importance of the young generation.

I do not believe the darkness has yet to fully comprehend the power that is held in their simple faith. But it has acted quicker to the words of Christ regarding the importance of this generation, and has unleashed dark torrents to capture their minds and imaginations. The religious feel they are accomplishing much through protection, by trying, fruitlessly, to shield these youngsters from the world they live in. In reality, they have simply numbed a generation to an encounter with Christ through religious requirements.

Dead tradition fears imagination at all costs. Afraid of what temptations could be released through the arts. We have attempted to stifle feelings of passion and desire, afraid that they will give way to lust and greed, creating a pathway for the enemy.

The darkness has engulfed a generation holding the

Taking Back the Night

very seeds that God has planted. It has opened doors to the supernatural in more extreme measures than most Pentecostal churches. It welcomes art in all of its varying forms – dance, painting, sculpture, film, music.

I do not fear desire; it has been placed there to create intimacy with our God. When we run from desire, we cut ourselves off from true intimacy with our Creator. Is there the possibility for sin to creep in? Yes, there always has been. God has always left that door open, because it defines our true love for Him. In our denial and death of self, is an act of love and intimacy.

Every day that Adam chose to walk in the garden with the Lord instead of tasting the forbidden fruit, he was defining his love. The very fact that the forbidden was there allowed Adam the opportunity to deny it. Does that mean we allow ourselves to get into situations where we are saturated in sin, yet stay abstained to prove greater love for Christ? Absolutely not! I have found that in this world you never have to go looking for temptation. We do not engulf ourselves in sin to prove our devotion, nor do we castrate our feelings to hide from temptation.

DEAD TRADITION FEARS IMAGINATION AT ALL COSTS

We embrace God, and learn to love and grow. That is the power of the fruits of the Spirit.

I have seen that the darkness, overzealous to pervert what God birthed, can only take them so far. A generation is coming full circle. They have experienced the fullness of what the world can give them, and they have found themselves standing at the church's door. For too long we have kept that door shut.

Fear of the unknown, and religion, has kept us from

An Extreme Generation

allowing entry to this wild generation. But their cries have amassed at the gates of Heaven. They have stirred the hearts of those truly listening within the four walls of the church, and movement has begun.

We have seen the door crack, and with it a flood of God's artistic expression that will change the face of the Bride, if we let it.

One of the early nights of Club Retro, we had in a local 'screamo' band. I had never heard screamo, and didn't know it even existed. I remember standing at the front door to the club when the band started. I could not tell you I heard the music; it was more like I felt the music. It was drawing me in.

I entered the main room and stood in the middle, eyes closed as the music began to wash over me. I didn't know the lyrics, I didn't know the music, I had never heard the band, I didn't even know if they were Christians. But the Spirit of God was in the music – the raw, unfiltered, unrefined, intense sound of the heart of God. The only way that I have found to define it was, it was real. I had grown up on Christian music, where everything was prepackaged, sealed and safe. And here was this music, unpackaged, extreme, real.

It moved me. I found myself totally captured in the presence of God. It transformed me. It was only afterward that I found out they were all Christians. I couldn't even understand the lyrics, and I didn't need to.

In the Christian music industry, for far too long we have focused on the idea that the lyrics are everything. We could care less about the music and the sound; we just want to know how many times they say Jesus in the song.

In the secular market, the music is everything. The lyrics are good, but first, how does the music speak to me. I have found that there is worship that moves beyond the lyrics, beyond the song, and you get captured by the rhythm of the heart of God. He transcends the words and speaks straight into the heart.

Often when I lead worship, I ask that words be taken off the screen. Now I know the words on the screen are there for a variety of reasons: visitors, attendees, to simply be able to worship along. Yet how often are we simply regurgitating someone else's encounter with God. I know that there are seasons for songs, and some songs capture the heart and imagination of God. But what happens when you take words away? Forget visitors and trying to make an environment that is safe and welcoming. That may be good for building a club, but for transforming lives, the whole point is to draw people closer to God, not back for another Sunday.

When we take words away, we create vulnerability, transparency. No one else is going to put the words in your mouth for you; you must encounter God yourself. It creates an opportunity for true intimacy. My wife loves it when I write her a poem much more than when I read her someone else's. Mine doesn't have to be good, but it is much more real, honest, and personal. When we strip the words away from a song, and allow the music to speak, it can draw people to such a deep place with our Father.

When *Consecrated* came to make our first CD, our goal was this: we wanted something that was raw, intense and real. We didn't want a Christian version of our music; we wanted something that speaks to the heart.

Too Young to Fight?

I had a phone call from a parent recently asking about children's ministry. They said that they wanted to come to our church,

An Extreme Generation

but that our children's ministry was too extreme for them. They came one Sunday and saw children shaking on the floor, speaking in tongues, praying for each other. In the end, they just felt that their child was too young for all of that.

I am shocked to find that so many parents and churches feel this way about this young generation. They settle for teaching them Bible stories and playing games, while the devil is actively fighting for their hearts and minds.

I told this parent, the devil is not waiting for your child to get older before he attacks. He is attacking now! You cannot shelter your child from the attacks of the enemy; you can only equip them for battle.

God has given us weapons of warfare. The question is, are we willing to fight? When I mentioned this to some parents recently, they said that they didn't feel their child could fully grasp or understand the weapons God has given us.

> **YOU CANNOT SHELTER YOUR CHILD FROM THE ATTACKS OF THE ENEMY, BUT YOU CAN EQUIP THEM FOR BATTLE**

I used this analogy with them. When someone in the army is given a bazooka and sent into battle, they first take their position. They set up their weapon, check their environment, and make sure the area is clear. They wait for the rest of the men to get into position. They aim at the target. They wait for their orders to shoot. They aim, they wait, they aim, they wait, they aim, they wait. Then finally they get to attack, maybe.

When you place that same bazooka, fully loaded, into the hands of a child, stand back! They simply point and shoot, point and shoot, point and shoot. And the devil knows this.

Taking Back the Night

He is freaked out by this new generation; they are wild and unhindered.

As adults, we wait so long before we attack, that most of the time the enemy has either moved or we have talked ourselves out of the fight. Not children. You put a weapon in their hand and they want to use it. I have three kids, and anything that vaguely resembles a sword, becomes a sword. Everything is a weapon in their hands. The devil has figured that out. Why do you think he has taken the time to pour so much into them in the world?

Look at this, the top entertainer in Australia last year was not Nicole Kidman, it was not Russell Crowe. It was The Wiggles. Four preschool teachers who have a TV show on the Disney channel. These four teachers have had the top concert tour the last two years, beating some of the best acts in the world.

The world has grasped the importance of this young generation. They spend time, money and resourses on reaching them and capturing their hearts and minds. All the while the church has sat by and watched this budding generation being taken right from under our noses. We have tried to maintain with religion, when that was never supposed to be in our arsenal. We should be giving them an encounter.

I have visited churches where you find their children's church hiding in some corner of the property. The room's a mess, the props are disgusting, and the children are still running around singing Father Abraham. We have downgraded the importance of a generation, and the devil has taken that for granted.

The top selling restaurant in all of America is McDonalds, a fast food store that focuses on children. Some of the top selling CD's in the music industry last year came from a little show

An Extreme Generation

called *High School Musical*, on Disney, for children.

How could we possibly be missing pouring into this great generation? In my years of children's ministry, I found that most children's pastors were beat down, discouraged, alone, and frustrated. This was not because they worked with children. I truly believe that those who work with young people and children are on the front lines of battle.

The devil does not have to attack a whole generation. All he has to do is attack the leaders. If he can keep the leaders beat down, defeated, and isolated, then he keeps the potential of these mighty warriors away from his gates. The devil knows that what God has to offer is amazing. He knows that it is real. He is freaked out at the thought of a massed army of young people – children, youth and young adults – who simply believe and operate in the supernatural.

So the devil has an all out attack on its leaders. He keeps churches in competition, rather than working together in unity. He invented a tier structure that has somehow been implemented in churches: children's ministry is the lowest and you work your way up to the adults. This is backwards thinking. It is deception thinking.

The very faith that this young generation has, when realized and breathed into, is infectious. It can jump-start the supernatural, and speak life into a dead body of religion. They simply believe. No questions, no doubt, just simple faith.

THE DEVIL IS SCARED OF THE FAITH OF A BELIEVING GENERATION

Scary Faith

We so often try to work it into something greater than it has

Taking Back the Night

to be. One morning when my daughter, Meaghan, was six, she blew me away. I had suffered for days with a filling that was loose in my mouth. I knew that a cavity had formed underneath it, but I dreaded going to the dentist. One morning, I had had enough and called the dentist and set up an appointment. As I was getting ready to leave, my daughter asked where I was going. When I told her what was wrong with my mouth, she set down her cereal spoon, walked over, simply placed her hands on each side of my face and prayed. Not a long prayer – a simple prayer. Then she walked back to her marshmallow cereal and kept eating. My first thought was, how sweet. I was extremely condescending, until I closed my mouth and realized that all pain was gone. I went to the dentist that morning anyway and had everything checked out. There was no cavity, nothing. In fact, other small cavities I used to have were completely gone, shocking the dentist. Simple faith.

This is not just the children though. I have found that all of this extreme generation, when they get saved from the world, have the same sort of belief. They have a much better understanding of the supernatural than I ever did. It does not shock them that there is healing or the prophetic. Why would they believe in something that does not have some element of the supernatural? I have found it harder to move in the supernatural with Christians who have never experienced healing than with someone not saved. So often we Christians struggle with our heads, while those lost in the world are longing to believe.

The devil has this knowledge. He is scared of the faith of a believing generation that is no longer hindered by the rules of religion. He does not know how to combat a generation that has learned to die to itself; it steals his ammunition away, so he has been trying different strategies. He continues to attack the

An Extreme Generation

leaders, and ostracizes the ministries that dare take the bold steps to invade the darkness.

When our church chose to embrace Club Retro, we did not do so without cost. Our church instantly had people leaving. There were those who left because they could not understand the concept of seeing people saved. And there were others who were set on seeing the Club close, and made that their mission. While scores of young people were being saved, they were blinded by the enemy and determined to see this ministry shut down.

The leaders and senior pastors had to decide: God is calling us to invade the darkness, and call forth this generation, no matter the cost. We went through a whole season of attack from within. I remember meeting with one of our members and his wife for dinner. Sitting in this restaurant, these friends shared with us a vision. The wife looked at me and said that I needed to repent for allowing satan into the church. That I needed to shut the doors and cleanse the building of the evil that had been welcomed in. These were friends. These were people we had relationship with.

My wife and I went through seasons where we felt completely alone on the front lines, alone in a boat in the middle of the water pulling up these fish. Does that sound like prophesy being fulfilled? Yet, we had a covering that supported us, and the attacks of the enemy did not succeed from the inside, so the devil tried a different strategy.

One cool day in late October, my wife and I were out running errands when I get a call that someone from the county had just dropped off a letter saying that Club Retro had ten days to close its doors or face fines. Surely, I thought, this must be a mistake, someone got something wrong. But it was no mistake. The

Taking Back the Night

county was closing down Club Retro for various wild reasons.

I spent the next ten days visiting every county office, trying to get in touch with the code enforcers, the permit offices, our county supervisor, all to no avail. Our county representative would not even meet with us. In one crazy meeting, ten members of the county met with me, and said that rock music could not be worship music. Worship music, they said, is what takes place in a good normal church on Sunday mornings. Our music cannot be worship – it is too loud.

I even had a code enforcement agent tell me that he would rather have children on the streets, committing crimes, than in our building. What was going on? I didn't understand, and I was running out of time to fight back. Did we pray? Absolutely. And we also took action. We held a silent protest in front of Club Retro, trying to get the attention of our county supervisor.

What was going to be a hundred young people lining the street in front of our church, turned into over six hundred young people – church members and community members. Radio stations showed up; news stations showed up. I started receiving letters of support from the local community in truck loads. The owner of the most liberal paper in Sacramento sent me a letter supporting Club Retro. He said that his son had attended our club many times and it had impacted his life. DJ's from local radio stations sent in their support. Local record stores, food stores, businesses sent in their support.

It wasn't long after this, that a nationally syndicated talk show put our story on the air, backing the cause of Club Retro. In the end, what the devil intended for evil, God used for good. And the devil ended up frustrated, agitated, and a loser. Light was shining, the darkness was fading, and the warriors were amassing.

- 23 -

THE FOREVER GENERATION

When I was in Bible College, I did an impromptu poll. I wanted to know how many of those who attended the Bible College were saved as a young person, and did not fall away from God in their walk. What I found shocked me. Over 75% had experienced a season of walking away from their faith and living a lifestyle of sin.

Then I began to talk to pastors – youth pastors, children's pastors. I found that the majority of them had the expectation that young people would fall away from God somewhere in their teen or young adult years. Their hope was to infill them with enough God, so that eventually they would come back to Him after their season of free-living was over.

Is that God's ultimate plan of salvation? Do all have to fall away? These questions plagued me. I was frustrated with the religious mindset that had already conceded this young generation to the enemy – the darkness has the fun, the darkness has the mystery. All we have to offer them is the potential for something later?

Taking Back the Night

What we must first do is break off these preconceived notions, the lies of the enemy. I do not believe our Lord is into one night stands. I call them 'camp experiences' – these once a year getaways where we *plan* a supernatural encounter with the Lord. I believe that when we foster supernatural, intimate encounters with the Lord on a regular basis, we create an environment that invites a deeper level of intimacy. It is in that place that these young ones become truly founded in Christ.

Does that mean they will never sin? Probably not, and I don't even think that is the point. The point is not perfection; the point is brokenness. Where do they go when they struggle? That is the point. They need to continue to run to Christ.

When we can create an environment where they feel safe running to Christ, rather than condemnation, then we can help foster lifestyles of radical Christian living. Instead, we have created such a level of fear of judgment, and of consequences. Is this the heart of God? I do not believe so. Is there a place to hold each other accountable for our actions? Absolutely, but in a family you do not ostracize a member for imperfection; otherwise, my family would be very lonely. What we need to do is learn to grow, encourage and help one another.

A call has gone out in the Spirit for the mothers and fathers, for the teachers and preachers, for the mentors and leaders to begin speaking into the 'forever' of this generation. To see the power and potential in a generation that has such intimacy with God that they do not turn away. To breathe life and speak prophetically into this generation a 'forever' mindset that has been forgotten and allowed to fall to the wayside.

PART 6
SHINE

Light does not simply shine, it invades.

- 24 -

BECOMING AN EXTREMIST

Billy Graham once published a letter that was written by a young communist to his girlfriend, breaking off their relationship because of his dedication to the communist cause. This letter so stirred me. Many times I have agitated some of my friends, because on days off, all I can talk about is God and church, what they call work. I told a good friend one day, this work, this God, He is my hobby, He is my job, He is my joy. I have nothing else I enjoy more than Him. I am constantly thinking about Him, and all that surrounds Him. Please do not ask me to stop pursuing Him. When I read this letter from this young communist, something jumped in me.

Below is the letter. See if his passions, albeit misrouted, resonate in you:

> "We communists have a high casualty rate. We are the ones who get shot and hung and ridiculed and fired from our jobs and in every other way made as uncomfortable as possible. A certain percentage of us get killed or imprisoned. We live in virtual poverty. We turn back to the party every penny we make above

Taking Back the Night

what is absolutely necessary to keep us alive.

We communists do not have time or the money for many movies or concerts or t-bone steaks or decent homes or new cars. We've been described as fanatics. We are fanatics! Our lives are dominated by one great, overshadowing factor: the struggle for world communism. We have a philosophy of life which no amount of money could buy. We have a cause to fight for, a definite purpose in life. . . .

There is one thing in which I am in dead earnest about, and that is the communist cause. It is my life, my business, my religion, my hobby, my sweetheart, my wife, my mistress, my bread and meat.

I work at it in the daytime and dream of it at night. Its hold on me grows, not lessens, as time goes on; therefore, I cannot carry on a friendship, a love affair, or even a conversation without relating it to this force which both drives and guides my life.

I evaluate people, looks, ideas, and actions according to how they affect the communist cause, and by their attitude toward it.

I've already been in jail because of my ideals, and if necessary, I'm ready to go before a firing squad." (Billy Graham sermon, "Mission Commitment", 1957)

Becoming An Extremist

There is a generation that has awakened, and they are desperate and passionate and they long for something that is real. Christ is real. His promises are real. The darkness has baulked at the light one too many times, and it is ready for an invasion.

I have found myself thinking about the song, *This Little Light of Mine*. It's a children's song, and I don't want to read too much into the fact that we call it a 'little light'. Yet, we have programmed ourselves to a false understanding of the light that is in us, this light that shines.

I cannot imagine it as a little light, nicely sitting on top of a safe candle, flickering gently in a soft breeze. This does not represent the light of Christ that is inside of me. The light in me is a raging fire that is burning and alive and longing to consume.

Before becoming a pastor, my father was a fireman with the Air Force. He would talk a lot about the process of controlled burns, or practice fires. These would be training exercises, where they would burn a field, or some brush, both in an attempt to make the area safe if a fire breaks out, and to practice on real fire. The problem is, he would tell us, no one ever told the fire that this was a practice. As far as the fire was concerned it was real.

He always told me growing up, there is no such thing as a safe fire. It is the same with the fire that is in us. In our attempt to control this fierce blaze, we have simply put it out. We have cut off the breath of God that breathes life into the Spirit of God in man. Yet, when we unleash the Spirit of God to consume us, all that is around us will experience the heat of the flame.

It reminds me of what C.S. Lewis wrote about Aslan in *The Lion, the Witch, and the Wardrobe*. He is good, but He is not safe.

For us to truly shine bright, we must open the door for that fire to burn in us.

- 25 -

MATCHLESS POTENTIAL

One day I was talking with God about why we have failed for so long in igniting the world around us. God had given me this vision of the world around me. It was dry. The land was parched; it was prime for someone to simply drop a match and ignite the world ablaze.

Growing up in California, we learn the danger of just one match. Just one spark, one match, can start a fire that consumes hundreds of acres. It is the same in the Spirit. I began to cry out to God: give us the simple spark to ignite the world around us! Then God showed me something new.

I had found a box of wooden matches. I pulled one out and began to look it at, and then I began to weep. I remember taking that little wooden match and putting it in my wallet. As I traveled around God would say, "Now, Matt, drop it now." So I would pull the match out of my wallet and drop it on the ground. I dropped this match on dry and parched areas. I dropped the match in the middle of cities. I dropped the match in the middle of fields. Every time I dropped it, I would weep. I was finally beginning to understand what God was saying.

Then one day, He asked me to drop it in a service, while I was speaking in a church. When I did, I picked back up the match and I showed it to everyone. I told them, this is the most pathetic thing in the world. I held it up high so that all of them could see this little match. Then I repeated, this is the most pathetic thing in the world.

Why? This match has all the potential of being a fire-starter. It has had all the potential of starting world-changing blazes. It has been in the middle of prime opportunity to affect all that is around it. It was created with purpose and destiny. It was supposed to shine. It was supposed to set things on fire. That was its purpose. Yet, just because it has this purpose does not mean it is ever going to fulfill it.

I had taken that match to all of these places where it could potentially do much more than just light. It could have been the match to go down in history, but instead, it was just another match that would never be anything. Just because it was a match, did not mean it would ever encounter something that would strike it. Something that would ignite its potential.

We have done the same thing. We have the potential to be fire-starters, the potential to set the world ablaze. God places us in the best possible situations to allow us to change the course of all humanity. But because we fear an encounter with the Lord, we have never been ignited.

What sets a match on fire? It is an encounter with the strike pad, something usually a bit rough and abrasive that can rub it just the right way and bring the friction that ignites the flame. We need to welcome encounters with God that will grow us and develop us, and yes, they may be abrasive, they may rub us

Matchless Potential

the wrong way, and that may be just what we need to ignite a revival that will not just fill buildings, but transform the world around us.

- 26 -

THE ARMY IS RISING

The darkness is waiting. The dawn of a new day is coming. The warrior Bride is awakening. Like Elijah, I hear the sounds of the coming rain, the coming fulfillment of promise. And I am stirred all the more.

How will this army amass? How will these fires be stoked?

In Ezekiel 37, the prophet is brought to the valley of dry bones. A valley that had once been filled with potential. Now it is desolate and dead. Filled with the remains of what once was, remains of old promises unfulfilled. Remains of shattered dreams, of what could have been.

God asks Ezekiel, son of man, can these bones live? And Ezekiel replies, God, only you know.

God is putting the fate of what is, in the hands of his Bride, the awakened ones, and asking us, can this church live? Will the darkness be allowed to dwell for another generation? Will there not be one, who will stand and shine in the midst of the night?

We have the opportunity to turn to Christ and say, "You

know, God! And we know your heart. Your heart is life and life more abundantly."

God is saying, speak to these dry bones and speak life.

I am tired of cursing the church. Am I happy with all that we have done in the last years? No, but I am not happy with all that *I* have done in the last years either. I am not on a crusade to kill church as we know it. I believe that we have a God who is into transforming. We need the church, just as we need the dry bones.

Those dry bones were the army that Ezekiel needed. Those dry bones were the destiny and the future for a nation. Those same dry bones are the destiny for a dying world. I will not curse those dry bones, but I will say to you, Life! Life! LIVE!

The time has come that we as Christians stop fighting with one another over the dead scraps that we have lived on for too long, and begin to speak destiny over those things we have forgotten to believe in. It is time that we awaken to the cry of the night and rise up and fight!

Together, we are the chosen generation. Let us not lose sight of our destiny, but let us passionately pursue in unity what is rightfully ours. The decision is ours; the promise is in our hands. Let us speak the words of longing that echo in the chambers of our God, and fill His heart with joy and release His glory on this land.

No longer can we be placated with false fulfillment and organized programs. Let us encourage one another and spur each other on for more, for something greater here and now.

What ultimately brought breath into that vast army Ezekiel saw, was an encounter with God. Right now we are in need of a supernatural encounter with God that will breathe on the Bride. It is that breath that will stoke the fire and cause an

The Army Is Rising

outbreak of the supernatural like we have never seen before.

I often think back to the young man with the Mohawk and the tattoos, sitting with me in front of Club Retro. His desperate plea was to encounter something real. I truly believe that his heart cry was the cry that God longs to see answered from the mouths of everyone who calls themselves a believer. Long for something real, something life-changing, something life-invading.

I made his desperation, his cry, my own, and in that journey I discovered truth, I discovered life. A life that was not my own – a life that required death.

It wasn't long after my pursuit of the true heart of God that I received a letter from a young man. This young man did not attend youth every Wednesday, but Club Retro had become his church. He wrote that his parents had divorced not long ago, and that his whole world had turned upside down. He said that he felt hurt, angry and on the verge of suicide. The situation left him feeling unwanted and unloved.

Both his parents had attended church. He had been to church himself, but he said that he needed something real. Sound familiar?

Some friends had invited him to Club Retro to see a death metal band play. The last thing that he had expected was for it to be at a church. It was there that he encountered God. When he met me, coming through the line, he experienced the supernatural presence of God and it impacted him, without any words being spoken. It hit him like a power line and it began to transform him. And he wanted more. He wrote that when he had looked at me, he had seen the true presence of God.

That night he went into our spiritual readings room. He

Taking Back the Night

had been sitting close to the room so he could hear what was going on. He didn't know about prophecy; he only knew that here was something real. He was drawn in by desire, and that night God encountered him and it changed his life. Now he had tasted something real, and he still wanted more.

What is this supposed to look like? It is that tangible, manifest presence of God. It happens when we don't even know it, but when we allow it to shine through us. It takes us not being satisfied, not being content with what we have today, what we have experienced thus far, but longing for more, longing for the promises of God to be fulfilled. It happens when we lay hold of the promises of God and with tenacious vigor, we don't let go.

Today I would not have to convince the Mohawk man about the power of my Jesus. I would simply introduce Him and expect.

The army is rising. We are standing on the cusp of the night and we are declaring that we are coming to fight. We are the Bride, and we are laying hold of our right! Warriors, no longer be timid, no longer be satisfied. You can hear the vibration of fear from the darkness – it senses the light, but it does not understand it. Yet it knows an invasion will bring it to its knees. Let us, warriors, hold back no longer. We must engage the darkness, we must take back the night!

Matthew and Siobhan Oliver live in Rocklin, California and have three beautiful children – Meaghan, Brigha, and Evan. Matthew and Siobhan are senior pastors at the Family Church in Roseville, where their heart and passion is to see the Kingdom of God established in their region. Matthew is currently working on his children's book *The Donkey and the Flea* and his tween series *The Wickers*.

If you would like to contact Matthew or Siobhan to come and minister, please visit:
    www.MatthewROliver.com *or*

or call the Family Church office at (916) 791-7555

To send Matthew an email please send it to:
    matthewroliver@msn.com

To send a letter to Matthew:
    Attention: Matthew Oliver
    The Family Church
    1529 Eureka Rd.
    Roseville, CA 95677

The Family Church website is:
    www.JointheFamily.net

Made in the USA
San Bernardino, CA
17 January 2014